W9-BRQ-563

Uncivil Liberties

Books by Calvin Trillin

Floater

Alice, Let's Eat

Runestruck

American Fried

U.S. Journal

Barnett Frummer Is an Unbloomed Flower

An Education in Georgia

Uncivil Liberties

C A L V I N   T R I L L I N

TICKNOR & FIELDS

NEW HAVEN AND NEW YORK: 1982

SOUTH HUNTINGTON PUBLIC LIBRARY
2 MELVILLE ROAD
HUNTINGTON STATION, NEW YORK
11746

973.92
TRI
817
T

Copyright © 1982 by Calvin Trillin

All rights reserved. No part of this work may be reproduced or transmitted in any form or by any means, electronic or mechanical, including photocopying and recording, or by any information storage or retrieval system, except as may be expressly permitted by the 1976 Copyright Act or in writing by the publisher. Requests for permission should be addressed in writing to Ticknor & Fields, 383 Orange Street, New Haven, Connecticut 06511.

The pieces included in this book first appeared as columns in *The Nation.*

Designed by Sally Harris / Summer Hill Books

Library of Congress Cataloging in Publication Data

Trillin, Calvin.
Uncivil liberties.
Columns from the Nation.
1. United States—Politics and government—1977–1981—Anecdotes, facetiae, satire, etc.
2. United States—Politics and government—1981– —Anecdotes, facetiae, satire, etc.
I. Nation (New York, N.Y.:1865) II. Title.
E872.T74 973.92′0207 81-18196
ISBN 0-89919-097-9 AACR2

Printed in the United States of America

D 10 9 8 7 6 5 4 3 2 1

To Robert Bingham

Contents

Uncivil Liberties

INTRODUCTION: The Years with Navasky

When I was approached about writing a column for *The Nation,* I asked for only one guarantee: Would I be allowed to make fun of the editor? When it comes to civil liberties, we all have our own priorities.

The editor, one Victor S. Navasky, responded to this question with what I believe the novelists call a nervous chuckle. In an editor's note introducing the first piece, he announced that I would be writing a "humor column"—apparently figuring that the readers would then assume that anything I said about him was meant as a joke. Since Navasky had once been the editor of an occasional publication called *Monocle, A Journal of Political Satire,* he presumably realized that writing a "humor column" would mean wrestling with what I have always thought of as The (Harry) Golden Rule: In modern America, anyone who attempts to write satirically about the events of the day finds it difficult to concoct a situation so bizarre that it may not actually come to pass while his article is still on the presses. The rule is named after Harry Golden because in the late fifties, when he realized that the white people in the part of North Carolina he lived in seemed to mind sitting down with black people but not standing up with them, he suggested that the schools be integrated through the simple device of removing the chairs. As I remember, he called his scheme the Harry Golden Plan for Vertical Integration. Not long after he proposed it, some libraries in the state were ordered by a federal court to desegregate, and they responded by removing their chairs.

In other words, when Jimmy Carter countered the threat of a Russian "combat brigade" in Cuba by having the Marines stage an assault landing on our own base at Guantanamo or when Ronald Reagan appointed as Deputy Secretary of State a man who could not name the Prime Minister of South Africa, some Sunday newspaper satirist somewhere in America was groaning at having his joke ruined by the legally constituted authorities. Someone who writes what has been officially labeled a "humor column" about the American scene lives in constant danger of being blindsided by the truth.

Why did I involve myself in such an unpromising enterprise? My first mistake, many years ago, was an involvement with *Monocle* and its editor, the same Victor S. Navasky. In those days, when we were all young and optimistic, I used to assure Navasky that the lack of a sense of humor was probably not an insurmountable handicap for the editor of a humor magazine. (He always responded with a nervous chuckle.) As an editor, after all, he was exacting. During the New York newspaper strike of 1963, *Monocle* published a parody edition of the *New York Post,* then as predictable in its liberalism as it was later to become in its sleaziness, and I suggested as the front-page headline "Cold Snap Hits Our Town; Jews, Negroes Suffer Most." Navasky refused to use the headline merely because there was no story inside the paper to go with it—

a situation that a less precise thinker might have considered part of the parody. Even then, I must say, Navasky's hiring policies seemed erratic—particularly his appointing as advertising manager a high-minded young man who found advertising so loathsome and digusting that, as a matter of principal, he refused to discuss the subject with anyone. What was most memorable about Victor S. Navasky at *Monocle,* though, was his system of payment to contributors—a system derived, according to my research, from a 1938 chart listing county-by-county mean weekly wages for Gray Ladies. My strongest memory of *Monocle* is receiving a bill from Navasky for a piece of mine the magazine had published—along with a note explaining that the office expenses for processing the piece exceeded what he had intended to pay me for it.

In the late sixties, *Monocle* folded. I wasn't surprised. My assurances to Navasky about his not needing a sense of humor had been quite insincere. Also, I had once observed the advertising manager's reaction to being phoned at the *Monocle* office by a prospective advertiser: "Take a message," he hissed at the secretary, as he bolted toward the door. "Tell him I'm in the bathroom. Get rid of him." Then, only about ten years later, Navasky fetched up as the new editor of *The Nation.* It was difficult for me to imagine that he would dare pay Gray Lady rates at a magazine of national reputation—even a money-losing magazine of national reputation. (Historians tell us that *The Nation* was founded many years ago in order to give a long succession of left-wing entrepreneurs the opportunity to lose money in a good cause.) *The Nation,* after all, had always railed against bosses who exploit workers. Still, it was among writers for radical journals that I most often heard the folk phrase "There's no goniff like a left-wing goniff." I thought about Navasky's stewardship of *Monocle* for a while, and then sat down to write him a letter of congratulations on being named editor of *The Nation.* It said, in its entirety, "Does money owed writers from *Monocle* carry over?" I received no reply.

I realize that this history with Navasky is one reason for some speculation by scholars in the field about the sort of negotiations that could have led to my agreeing to do a column for *The Nation.* ("If he got caught by Navasky twice, he must be soft in the head.") The entire tale can now be told. The negotiations took place over lunch at a bar in the Village. I picked up the check. I had asked Navasky beforehand if he minded my bringing along my wife, Alice. I figured that she would be a reminder that I was no longer the carefree young bachelor who barely complained about being stiffed regularly by the *Monocle* bookkeepers, but a responsible married man with two daughters and an automatic washer-dryer combination (stack model). Navasky, the cunning beast, said Alice would be most welcome. He knew her to be a sympathetic soul who somehow saw a connection in his saving money on writers and the possibility that he might buy a new suit.

Once we had our food, Navasky made his first wily move. He suggested two very specific ideas for regular columns I might be interested in writing for *The Nation*—both of them of such surpassing dumbness that I long ago forgot precisely what they were. One of them, it seems to me, was on the practical side—a weekly gardening column, maybe, or a column of auto repair hints.

"Those are the silliest ideas I ever heard," I said, with relief. "The only column I might like to do is so far from Wobbly horticulture, or whatever you have in mind, that I don't mind mentioning it because you obviously wouldn't be interested—a thousand words every three weeks for saying whatever's on my mind, particularly if what's on my mind is marginally ignoble." As long as I was safe from an agreement, I thought I might as well take advantage of one of those rare opportunities to say "ignoble" out loud.

"It's a deal," the crafty Navasky said, putting down the hamburger I was destined to pay for and holding out his hand to shake on the agreement. Caught again.

"I hate to bring up a subject that may cause you to break out in hives," I said, "but what were you thinking of paying me for each of these columns?" I reminded him of the responsibilities of fatherhood and the number of service calls necessary to keep a stack-model washer-dryer in working order.

"We were thinking of something in the high two figures," Navasky said.

I remained calm. The sort of money we were discussing, after all, was already a step up from *Monocle* rates. The only check I ever received from *Monocle*—for presiding over a panel discussion in an early issue—was for three dollars. ("Well, it's steady," I said when Navasky later asked if I would run similar discussions as a monthly feature of *Monocle*. "A person would know that he's got his thirty-six dollars coming in every year, rain or shine, and he could build his freelance on that.") Still, I felt a responsibility to do some negotiating.

"What exactly do you mean by the high two figures?" I said.

"Sixty-five dollars," Navasky said.

"Sixty-five dollars! That sounds more like the middle two figures to me. When I hear 'high two figures,' I start thinking eighty-five, maybe ninety."

"You shook on it," Navasky said. "Are you going to go back on your word right in front of your own wife?"

I looked at Alice. She shrugged. "Maybe Victor'll buy a new suit," she said.

I called for the check.

A few weeks after I began the column, Navasky asked me if William Henry Harrison's Secretary of State had ever said what I had quoted him as saying.

"At these rates, you can't always expect real quotes, Victor," I said, preferring to leave it at that.

As it happens, the only quotation in these columns whose authenticity has been the subject of any serious controversy is H. L. Mencken's 1928 prediction that the first President from the Deep South would have, among other attributes, "a charm comparable to that of the leading undertaker of Dothan, Alabama," and I'm pleased to say that it has proved to be, in its own way, quite genuine.

Of course, we all make mistakes. After I mentioned having read that the editor of *Playboy,* one Arthur Kretchmer, made $520,734 a year, *The Nation* received a letter from a *Playboy* associate editor named Asa Baber pointing out that my source for the figure had turned out to be in error, and chastising me for not checking with Kretchmer before printing an account of his embarrassing wealth—checking with the subject being, in Baber's words, "an old tradition in journalism." Naturally, I was happy to set the record straight in the letter column of *The Nation,* and I'm happy to do so here: Despite what you may read in this book, Arthur Kretchmer makes $165 a week, plus time and a half for overtime. The annual salary of Asa Baber is $520,734.

I must admit that in these columns I haven't made a fetish of the old traditions of journalism—the tradition, for instance, of covering events only when they actually occur. In the winter of 1979, Navasky asked me why I was beginning to cover the Great Presidential Debates between Edward Kennedy and Ronald Reagan months before either party had decided on a candidate.

"I'm trying to get a jump on the other fellows," I said. "They all have expense accounts."

I have taken Navasky's handshake to mean that I am also free from whatever traditions journalism might retain in the area of fairness and civility—although I have, of course, tried to give Navasky himself every benefit of the doubt. I don't mean that I was ever a strict believer in what used to be known as objective journalism, the best definition of which I heard from a photographer in Little Rock who told me, "Before I go out to take a picture of someone, I just stop at the city desk and say, 'Do you want him gazing out toward the sunset or picking his nose?' " As a reporter, though, I have at least aspired to the standard of objectivity we used to make do with on the college paper—"We strive to be equally inaccurate about both sides."

A commentator, I learned, labors under no such restrictions. "Do you really think that's fair?" Alice said one day, after reading a manuscript in which I had made some base and underhanded statement about the Governor's girlfriend or the President's appearance or the Secretary of State's mental health.

"Not in the least," I said, putting the manuscript into an envelope for delivery to *The Nation*. "Not in the least."

* * *

I have done some tinkering here and there, but basically the pieces in this book appear as they appeared in *The Nation,* in chronological order. I would like to thank the members of *The Nation*'s editing staff, who seemed particularly alert to my needs after I admitted publicly in an early column that I had never mastered the spelling of "occurred." Any errors that may appear in this book should not be blamed on them, of course, but on Victor S. Navasky.

The Brightside

April 22, 1978

I was pleased that Dr. Norman Vincent Peale announced his intention to do a good-news radio program just as the Korean bribery scandal revealed to me the bright side of the war in Vietnam. It is so rarely that Dr. Peale and I have the opportunity to march in step. Because we lost the war in Vietnam, the Tongsun Park hearings had made me realize, we will not have to spend billions of dollars propping up a government in Saigon that, once having mastered the democratic process, would spend part of those billions bribing our Congressmen to assure the steady flow of more billions. If the Vietnamese want to bribe someone with his own money from now on, they'll just have to bribe the Russians.

In case Norman Vincent Peale requires further evidence of what good news our defeat in Vietnam really was, he need only contemplate the presence in our country of another triple-handled man of God—the Rev. Sun Myung Moon. The Reverend Moon is Korean—just one more result of our shortsightedness in not permitting ourselves to be, as they used to say in the fifties, pushed into the sea at Pusan. We were fortunate in having General Westmoreland and that crowd running our side the next time around. Now that we have been pushed into the air over the

American Embassy in Saigon, we need not worry that in ten or fifteen years some Vietnamese industrialist will proclaim himself the Messiah and then snatch Scarsdale clean of clear-eyed youths in order to build a New World Order of candy-peddlers and panhandlers.

I was tempted to abandon brightsidedness last week when I came across a remarkably prescient H. L. Mencken quotation that seems to have been making the rounds of Washington egg-head circles lately. In an essay that described Henry Grady's New South as "depressingly similar to the Old Middle-West," Mencken wrote, "On those dark moments when I fear that the Republic has trotted before these weary eyes every carnival act in its repertoire, I cheer myself with the thought that someday we will have a President from the deserts of the Deep South . . . The President's brother, a prime specimen of *Boobus Collumnus Rubericus,* will . . . gather his loutish companions on the porch of the White House to swill beer from the bottle and snigger over whispered barnyard jokes about the darkies. The President's cousin, LaVerne, will travel the Halleluyah circuit as one of Mrs. McPherson's soldiers in Christ, praying for the conversion of some Northern Sodom's most Satanic pornographer as she waves his work—well thumbed—for all the yokels to gasp at. . . . The President's daughter will record these events with her box camera. . . . The incumbent himself, cleansed of his bumpkin ways by some of Grady's New South hucksters, will have a charm comparable to that of the leading undertaker of Dothan, Alabama."

What bright side can one find in having to spend three

more years hearing incessantly about a First Family so predictable that it could be predicted in 1928? There is one: The President virtually never tells any cute stories about Amy. He has either restrained a strong parental instinct for the good of the nation, or Amy is the only nine-year-old alive without a trace of personal charm.

As the father of two charming daughters about Amy's age, I can imagine how difficult such restraint must be—even though I have never bothered to exercise it myself. I simply explain my excesses—my repetitions of Abigail's most telling punch lines, my rendition of Sarah's rendition of "I'm Don José from Far Rockaway"—by posting on the wall of my office a quotation from a President to whose incumbency the Carter administration is often compared, William Henry Harrison. (Oddly enough, Harrison had his own problems with the Middle East. It was his Secretary of State who caused a diplomatic incident by mumbling, as he emerged from a Cairo conference, "If there *were* inferior races, the Arabs would be one of them.") Harrison, so the story goes, replied to his wife's suggestion that he boasted too much about their daughter by saying, "Anyone who is not objectionable about his daughter is a pervert."

Once I had brightsided the Carters, I turned, in an even-handed fashion, to Governor Jerry Brown, of California. Brown is single. No daughters to date movie stars or sons to be photographed with Bianca Jagger. As far as I know, he does not even have any friends. A Brown Presidency, in other words, would be a sort of breathing spell for those of us who have been made by Bert Lance to wonder what

Holistic Heuristics

May 13, 1978

I've decided to skip "holistic." I don't know what it means, and I don't want to know. That may seen extreme, but I followed the same policy toward "Gestalt" and the twist, and lived to tell the tale.

"Aren't you even curious about what it means?" my wife, Alice, the family intellectual, asked me one day.

"No, I think I'll just give it a skip," I said. "Thanks anyway."

Alice had just finished comparing the East and West Coast definitions of "holistic" with a friend of ours who was visiting from California. Our friend—I'll call him Tab, although his name is, in fact, Bernard—had mentioned meeting the woman he now lives with in a hot tub that belonged to someone who practiced holistic psychology. (Now that I think of it, Tab may have said that the host practiced organic orthodontia; I only remember that it was one of the healing arts.) I should probably explain that a hot tub is a huge wooden vat in someone's backyard—back where the barbecue set used to be a long time ago. In California, I gathered from Tab, people who are only casually acquainted take off all of their clothes, climb into a hot tub together, and make up new words. I was later informed by a refugee from Beverly Hills that making up new words is not the only thing naked people do in hot tubs; in Southern California, he said, naked people in hot tubs sometimes snort cocaine while discussing real estate.

"How about 'heuristics'?" Alice asked.

"Is that the same word?" I said, thinking she might have hit me with a Boston pronunciation, just for laughs.

"Different word," Alice said. "But also very big these days."

"I think I'll give that one a skip, too," I said. "Fair's fair."

I'm quick to acknowledge that, through no efforts of my own, I'm in a better position than most citizens to be cavalier about these matters. Having a family intellectual available, I can always arrange to have words like "holistic" or "heuristics" translated if it should prove absolutely necessary—if they turn up on a road sign, for instance, or on a menu or on a visa application. Also, the family intellectual in question happens to be very understanding about bearing the burden of keeping in touch with the language for the entire family. She knows how disappointed I was when I took the trouble to search out the accepted definition of "prioritize" only to find out that it didn't mean what I'd hoped it would mean.

I should make it clear that I have no objection to new words. I am, for instance, a regular user of the word "yucky"—which, as far as I can tell, was invented out of whole cloth by Oscar the Grouch. I have even invented a new word myself now and then—on long evenings, when there's nothing much on the tube. I was particularly proud of finding a new word to replace awkward phrases like "the woman he now lives with"—CeeCee was my word, from the old news magazine euphemism "constant companion"—but then Alice told me that CeeCee sounded like a breath mint.

What I have a resistance to is not new words but words that come into a vogue that may not last as long as the one for the twist—disappearing from the vocabulary of the sophisticates just about the time that a slow reactor like me has learned the difference between the East Coast and the West Coast definitions. I realize that passing up words like "holistic" may strike some people as laziness or even philistinism, but I have always liked to think of it as a sort of negative act of character. The speed of trends being what it is these days, after all, about the only way a citizen can exhibit an independent spirit is to remain totally inert.

When I'm trying to impress Alice, for instance, I remind her that I have resolutely ignored drinking fashions for twenty-five years, steadily knocking back Scotch whisky the entire time. They turned to wine; I drank Scotch. They smoked pot; I drank Scotch. They ordered Perrier water; I drank Scotch. They snorted cocaine while naked in a hot tub discussing real estate; I drank Scotch. I like to think that late on some Saturday nights Alice can point to me—slumped in the corner, sodden with Scotch—and say, "There sits a man of principle. Inert."

Signs of the Times

June 3, 1978

In the middle sixties, when those in charge realized rather suddenly that something really ought to be done to eliminate various sorts of discrimination against black people, the airlines got right in step: they started furnishing *Ebony* in the magazine racks of airliners. A few years later, when there was talk of the need for blacks to control their own institutions and businesses, the airlines were again in the vanguard: they added to the magazine racks a magazine called *Black Enterprise*.

As a regular user of the airlines, I can report that the supply of black passengers has not kept up with the supply of *Ebonys*. On a weekday businessmen's flight, I have occasionally watched with some interest as a white passenger—a drummer in electronic software, say, who has finished his reports and is bored with his historical novel about life in a pioneer Montana bawdyhouse and is still an hour and a half out of LaGuardia—strolls over to the magazine rack to see what is left to read. What is left at that stage of the flight is a stationery-and-writing kit, a kiddies' magazine with a name like *Puss 'n Boots,* three unthumbed copies of *Ebony,* and a pristine copy of *Black Enterprise*. The drummer gropes in the slots of the magazine rack for a while, presumably thinking that an undersized *Reader's*

Digest may have been overlooked. Then, empty-handed, he returns to his seat and tries to find something of interest in *Safety Instructions for Your Boeing 727.*

Occasionally, when I find myself bored and still an hour and a half out of LaGuardia, I conjure up in my mind the presence across the aisle of a visiting dignitary from Czechoslovakia, accompanied by two official escorts from the State Department. During the flight, the men from State have been filling the Czech in on the progress black Americans have made—using State Department sort of statistics, like how many Chevrolets each black steelworker in Gary is risking repossession on, and how many more black Ph.D.s there are in America than there are reindeer in all of Lapland. The Czech looks impressed, for a Czech. After a while, he stretches, stands, and strolls up the aisle of the plane toward the bathroom—leaving the State Department men with the glow of professional briefers who have just successfully briefed. The bathroom is occupied. Waiting in front of the magazine rack, the Czech idly reaches over to pick up the three remaining magazines. Suddenly, the State Department men realize what is happening. They rush up the aisle to stop him. Too late. He sees. He knows.

Any sign of corporate response to social problems is always welcome, of course. I read the Surgeon General's warning about cigarette smoking every chance I get. My favorite warning appeared on a Winston billboard that loomed over Times Square until recently. I used to offer a small prize—two vials of nicotine and an engraved sterling silver pillbox full of tar—to anyone who could stand with both feet on Broadway and read it unaided by binoculars or telescope. The prize was double for anyone who could do it with smoke in his eyes.

Lately, I have begun to notice a similar disclaimer on ads for the New York City Off-Track Betting operation. The original argument for off-track betting, as I remember it, was that, given the eternal truth that a certain number of people are going to take a flier on the horses no matter how many laws are passed against it, a government-controlled betting system would keep the bookie money out of the hands of wicked mobsters—and take a cut of the action for the citizenry at the same time. In my innocence, I assumed that the government would simply make off-track betting available for those who wanted it—in the discreet way a state liquor store in Vermont or Alabama makes liquor available. As it turns out, OTB spends thousands of dollars on subway and billboard advertisements to persuade citizens that betting on the horses will transform them into some combination of Frank Sinatra and Walt Frazier. These days, about the only way a responsible New York breadwinner can escape OTB ads imploring him to blow the rent money on the ponies is to go to the track. Recently, though, the Off-Track Betting Corporation added to its huge subway ads a small notation in the left-hand corner that says, "For information on the most effective treatment for the compulsive gambler, contact the National Council on Compulsive Gambling, 142 E. 29."

In a way, signs of corporate response to social problems are made even more interesting by the realization that the sign may, in fact, be the response. A couple of weeks ago, on an airline flight chock-full of people like drummers in electronic software, I noticed for the first time among the magazine-rack leftovers a magazine devoted to women in business. "Well, that takes care of that," I thought. "Next case." I now realize what the coal industry lobbyists who considered federal health-and-safety regulations unnecessary must have had in mind instead: a small, well-designed sign at the entrance to each mine saying, "Warning: Daily descent into this mine could result in the contraction of black lung and/or other occupational diseases."

Publisher's Lunch

June 24, 1978

I'm sorry that the editor of *The Nation,* one Victor S. Navasky, didn't ask me to participate in the symposium on publishing he ran in the June 3rd issue. I have a lot of ideas on the subject, many of them acquired in the course of doing research for a book I have been working on for many years—*An Anthology of Authors' Atrocity Stories About Publishers.* (So far, I have failed to find a publisher for the book, despite a friend of mine having improved the original idea considerably by proposing that the anthology be published as an annual.) I suppose Navasky thought that my only idea for reform of the publishing industry was the one I mentioned to him some years ago, when he was writing a column himself—before he wised up and became an editor. That idea was in the form of a simple regulation to be adopted by the industry: The advance for a book must be larger than the check for the lunch at which it was discussed.

At the time, as I remember, the publishers said my proposed regulation was unrealistic. What Navasky has failed to realize is that since the last time we discussed the subject I have figured out how to effect this and many other necessary reforms whether the publishers find them realistic or not—through the simple vehicle of New York City ordinances. Because the publishing industry is concentrated in Manhattan, its activities could be regulated by the City Council in the same way that taxi rates or building permits are regulated. I realize that any hint of regulation would cause the publishers to threaten a mass move to New Jersey—the way the Wall Street crowd threatened to move to New Jersey when the city hinted about imposing what amounted to a parasite tax on stock-and-bond transactions—but the threat would obviously never be carried out. Where would publishers eat lunch in New Jersey?

Some of the ordinances would be simple consumer protection. Any person furnishing a blurb for a book jacket, for instance, would be required to disclose his connection to the author of the book. A one-sentence parenthetical identification, supported by an affidavit filed in triplicate with the Department of Street Maintenance and Repair, would suffice. If, for example, a new novel by Cushman Jack Hendricks carried a blurb by a famous novelist named Dred Schlotz saying "Hendricks writes like an angel with steel in its guts," the blurb would simply be signed "Dred Schlotz (Drinking buddy at Elaine's)" or "Dred Schlotz (Hopes to be chosen shortstop on the author's team at next Easthampton writers' softball game)" or "Dred Schlotz (Just a fellow who likes to keep his name before the reading public between books)."

I suppose the publishers would put up some First Amendment quibble to the Open Blurb Law—in the same way that some civil liberties fanatics objected on First Amendment grounds to my plan to rid the city of stores with names like "Tshotchkes 'n' Things" through an ordinance that called for any shopkeeper who failed to spell out a conjunction to be put in the stocks. But what I propose is really no different from the truth-in-packaging legislation that requires, say, frozen-food manufacturers to list how much MSG and cornstarch the consumer will be eating if he thaws out what purports to be a spinach soufflé. Although there may be writers who believe their books to be different in spirit from a spinach soufflé, spiritual differences are not recognized by the Department of Consumer Affairs. In fact, as part of my research for *An Anthology of Authors' Atrocity Stories About Publishers,* I conducted a study (employing my usual controls) that showed the average shelf life of a trade book to be somewhere between milk and yogurt. It is true that some books by Harold Robbins or any member of the Irving Wallace family last longer on the shelves, but they contain preservatives.

One ordinance would require any novel containing more then 300 pages and/or fourteen major characters and/or three generations to provide in its frontis matter a list that includes the name of each character, the page of first mention, nickname or petname, and sexual proclivities. Under another ordinance, passed despite some opposition from an organization called Urban Neurotics United, each publisher would be limited to one Kvetch Novel per month ("A Kvetch Novel," in the language of the ordinance, "will be defined as any novel with a main character to whom any reader might reasonably be expected to say, 'Oh, just pull up your socks!' or 'Will you *please* quit kvetching?' ") All profits from books published by convicted felons who have held public office would, by law, be turned over to a fund that provides Gypsies with scholarships to Harvard Business School. An author will be legally prohibited from ending a book's Acknowledgments by thanking his wife for her typing. There would be no books by any psychotherapist who has ever appeared on a talk show. Each September, under the joint supervision of the Office of the Borough President of Staten Island and the Department of Marine Resources, the city itself would publish a book called *An Anthology of Authors' Atrocity Stories About Publishers*.

Usually Reliable Sources

July 22, 1978

Lately, I have been forced to invoke the name of Marie Torre almost once a week. Marie Torre, in one of the landmark cases involving a reporter's right to protect a source, went to jail rather than reveal which studio executive had told her that Judy Garland was getting too fat. She is our John Peter Zenger, West Coast Division. While invoking her name, I have given assurances that I too would be willing to go to jail rather than reveal my source, although I would prefer a suspended sentence.

What I have been asked to reveal is where I found a quotation attributed to H. L. Mencken which appeared in this space several weeks ago in a column that also included quotations credited to William Henry Harrison and William Henry Harrison's Secretary of State (I can never remember his name). In the passage quoting Mencken's contemplations on what the first President from the Deep South would be like, there was something uncomfortably prescient about his description of a brother who would "gather his loutish companions on the porch of the White House to swill beer from the bottle and snigger over barnyard jokes about the darkies" and a cousin on the Halleluyah circuit waving well-thumbed copies of pornographic magazines for the yokels to gasp at.

interview with *Playboy* magazine, the Presidential archives of the Carter administration. "If after the inauguration you find a Cy Vance as Secretary of State and Zbigniew Brzezinski as head of National Security, then I would say we've failed," Jordan said to the *Playboy* interviewer (who, as far as we know, was fully clothed), "And I'd quit. But that's not going to happen." When both Vance and Brzezinski were appointed, it was widely thought that Jordan's statement had been yet another example of those statements by Presidential aides, at once arrogant and dead wrong, that prove what scholars call The Haldeman Rule: "No nation has ever been wisely governed by advance men." As it turned out, though, Jordan had been prophetic: they have a Vance and Brzezinski, and, by the account of virtually all foreign policy analysts, they have failed. (Jordan has not quit, but nobody's predictions are perfect.) I have been informed that the problem between Brzezinski and the Georgians goes deeper than the *Playboy* quote. Apparently, during National Security Council meetings that take place before nine in the morning, the sight of one of Carter's Boys drinking a Coke with goobers in it causes Brzezinski to flash what some interpret as a condescending smile. It was not Mencken, I believe, but Ambrose Bierce who wrote, "Only a Southerner could be made to feel socially inadequate in the presence of a Pole."

I have decided, however, that it would not be a betrayal of Zbigniew Brzezinski, John Peter Zenger or Marie Torre to admit a mistake made in the column in question. The quotation credited to William Henry Harrison ("Anybody who is not objectionable about his daughter is a pervert") may have actually been said by Franklin Pierce. That, at least, is what I have been led to believe by a particularly zealous Piercist of my acquaintance. The undiplomatic quotation attributed to William Henry Harrison's Secretary of State ("If there were inferior races, the Arabs would be one of them") has not been questioned. My only regret is that I can't remember his name.

The New New Right

August 19, 1978

The emergence of a New Right may make some people feel uneasy; it just makes me feel long in the tooth. I happen to be old enough to remember the emergence of the New Right that emerged before this one. It emerged in 1961, at a time in our history when Stash Radziwill was Billy Carter and Dwight D. Eisenhower had just finished being Gerald Ford. Its resubmergence, I think, can be dated fairly precisely at the national elections of 1964, when Barry Goldwater, who said in his campaign that the use of American combat troops in Vietnam might be a possibility worth considering, was defeated by Lyndon B. Johnson, the last successful Democratic peace candidate in Presidential politics. It was not just a New Right but a Short Right.

Its meetings, though, were long. Those who referred to it as the Right Wing Renaissance were not making a comment on its style. Robert Welch, of the John Birch Society still holds the American record for uninterrupted monotone exposition. Billy James Hargis, it was said at the time, could bore the eyeballs right out of your head. The old New Right loved audio-visual aids; it loved verbatim quotations proving that international communism had discussed it plans for world conquest openly and at great length. The average public meeting of the Christian Anti-Communist Crusade seemed to break up just twenty or thirty minutes short of eternity. Speaker after speaker would go on about Khrushchev having said "We will bury you," and, sure enough, a member of the audience could almost feel the earth closing in over him. For weeks after a reporter had covered a meeting of the New Right, he could be moved to palpable enthusiasm by being assigned a story on Title Two housing or the quarterly figures on gross national product.

It took me a while to figure out why the New Right was so aggressively boring. The answer started to come to me during a century and a half I spent one day in 1961 at Harding College in Searcy, Arkansas, which produced a lot of the New Right's literature, as well as an array of audio-visual aids that included a plaster-of-Paris model of the American Way of Life. While I was listening to a remarkably detailed explanation of the plaster-of-Paris model of the American Way of Life, my thoughts turned to some way to explain just why the New Right was so mind-numbing—having wandered in that direction after some time attempting to recall the members of my sixth-grade class row by row and some relatively interesting moments trying to name all ten provinces of Canada. "As boring as this can't be any accident," I suddenly said to myself. "As boring as this must be policy."

The New Right, I knew, prided itself on a scholarly knowledge of Communist ideology and tactics. Being scholars, they must have realized that compared to an exposition by the average Communist Party theoretician an exposition by Robert Welch might remind some people of after-dinner conversation by Noel Coward. It was known by then why Communists in the thirties had found it so easy to outlast everyone until they became a majority in any meeting they wanted to take over: no one else could bear to sit through their speeches. By the early sixties, even Americans who had not made a study of the Red Menace had been given the opportunity to see Soviet trade exhibitions and World's Fair pavilions—those endless explanations of hydroelectric plants in Yakutsk. It did not require Herbert Philbrick to detect the underlying policy: the Soviets were engaged in a conscious conspiracy to bore the world into submission. The New Right obviously figured it would fight fire with fire.

Times have changed. Khrushchev has himself been buried. The noted women's magazine journalist Lee Radziwill was suddenly replaced by the noted women's magazine journalist Linda Byrd Johnson, who was herself supplanted by Julie Nixon. There is a new New Right. I intend to ignore it, on the off chance that its meetings have any similarity at all to the meetings of the old New Right. According to my calculations, another one ought to be along in 1994, and I might be ready to deal with it by then. Every other New Right is enough for anyone.

Incompatible, With One L

September 16, 1978

I married Alice under the assumption that she could spell "occurred." She now insists that nothing specific was mentioned about "occurred" in prenuptial discussions. It seems to me, though, that implicit in someone's making a living as a college English teacher is the representation that she is a speller with a repertoire adequate to any occasion. She must have known that the only person in her line of work I had any experience being related to, my Cousin Keith from Salina, once reached the finals of the Kansas state spelling bee. She now says Cousin Keith's spelling triumph was never spoken of between us. I distinctly remember, though, that I listed for Alice the highlights of our family's history, as any prospective bridegroom might for his future wife, and Cousin Keith has always been part of my standard Family History recitation—along with my Cousin Neil, who was once the head drum major of the University of Nebraska marching band, and my Uncle Benny Daynofsky, who in his early eighties was knocked down by a car while planting tomatoes in his own backyard in St. Jo. It is significant that she does not deny knowing about Uncle Benny.

Is spelling the sort of thing that modern young couples get straightened out beforehand in marriage contracts? I wouldn't bring it up after all of these years, except that, as it happens, I can't spell "occurred" either. I was forced to look it up twice in order to write the first paragraph, and once more to get this far in the second. Somehow, I had expected to marry someone whose spelling would be, if not perfect, at least complementary to mine. We would face the future with heads held high, and maybe a short song on our lips—confident that together we could spell anything they dished out. Before we had been married a month, the real world started to eat away at that fantasy: It turned out that Alice was not very good on "commitment." I don't mean she didn't have any; she couldn't spell it. I have never been able to spell "commitment" myself.

I know how to spell "embarrass"—usually considered by double-letter specialists to be a much more difficult word. I have been able to spell it for years. I planted "embarrass" in my mind at an early age through a rather brilliant mnemonic device having to do with barstools. In fact, not to make a lot out of it, I had always thought of my ability to spell "embarrass" as a nice little facility to bring to a marriage—the sort of minor bonus that is sometimes found in a husband's ability to rewire lamps. (I don't mean it was the only facility I was able to contribute: Although I can't rewire a lamp, I can bark like a dog and I can blow a hard-boiled egg out of its shell seven times out of ten.) We have now been married thirteen years, and Alice still has not asked me how to spell "embarrass." Apparently, she has a mnemonic device of her own. I have never inquired. That sort of thing doesn't interest me.

For a while, our reformist friends used to urge us to

make a list of the words that troubled both of us—their theory being that some wretched consistency in the American educational system would be further documented by the fact that a husband and wife who went to public schools 1,300 miles apart were left without the ability to spell precisely the same words. Not long ago, an analytically inclined Easterner who came over for a drink when Alice happened to be out of town tried to establish some psychological significance in which words Alice and I were able to spell and which ones we weren't. "Is it really an accident that neither of you can spell 'commitment' but both of you can spell 'embarrass'?" he said. It has been my experience that when analytically inclined Easterners ask a question that begins "Is it really an accident . . ." the answer is always yes. I wanted to write Alice to describe the psychological analysis of our spelling problem, but, as it happens, the one word she can spell and I can't is "cockamamie."

Converts to the new politics of lowered expectations have told me that I should simply accept Alice's spelling limitations and comfort myself with thoughts of the many splendid qualities she does have—the way Americans are now supposed to settle for only two gigantic automobiles, reminding themselves that some people in Chad have none at all. I have tried that. I have reminded myself that Alice can explain foreign movies and decipher road maps. I suspect that in a pinch she might be able to rewire a lamp. But, having come of drinking age in the 1950s, I may be culturally immune to the politics of lowered expectations. I can't get over the suspicion that a politician who preaches that doctrine is really arguing that we ought to settle for

Taxing Problems

October 7, 1978

With all of the talk recently about the property tax in California, I'm surprised that nobody is discussing my suggestion that hot tubs be taxed at a higher rate than flower gardens. For some reason, everybody wants to argue only about how high property taxes are, completely overlooking their potential as an instrument of public policy. For years, the property tax has remained philosophically dormant while the income tax laws expressed the values of the society. Allowing an income-tax deduction for mortgage interest, for instance, is obviously another way of saying that every man should have a castle—or two or three castles if he is able to pick up a deal on a beach house and scrapes up the down payment on a ski chalet. The ceiling on taxation of capital gains reflects the national belief that speculation is a more worthwhile way to make a living than work. The deduction for charitable contributions is simply the government's way of indicating that rich people are in a better position than poor people to decide which eleemosynary institutions are deserving of the taxpayers' support. Why else would coal miners be required to share the cost of a stockbroker's gift to the St. Paul's School's boat-house fund? The laws providing tax shelters reflect the strong philosophical commitment of the Founding Fathers, particularly Alexander Hamilton, to the principle that the public good would be served if dentists owned cattle ranches.

Although some cities offer property tax abatement as a way of attracting industry, the levy on residential property has never been widely recognized as anything except a device for raising funds to support the machinery of government—what less sophisticated societies would call a "tax." In fact, the lessons to be learned from the accidental social impact of the property tax run contrary to the teachings of the American Way of Life. Could it be, for instance, that the Founding Fathers, thrifty homeowners all, intended that a citizen be penalized through taxation for improving his property? Would Benjamin Franklin approve of an assessment system that undercut a man's incentive to provide his family with aluminum siding and weather stripping throughout? Is it really American to demand that the owner of the big house on the hill—a man whose tendency toward acquisition has been encouraged by income tax laws allowing him to depreciate over six years a Boeing 747 he owns in company with two dermatologists and a shopping-center czar—pay more than the shack dweller for the education of the town's children? The children of the owner of the big house on the hill are not even among those being educated: He is the stockbroker and they row on the 150-pound crew at St. Paul's School.

I first proposed that property tax be brought under social-policy planning several years ago at a tax symposium I held at Arthur Bryant's barbecue restaurant in Kansas City. Interestingly enough, there was a complete press blackout. To be fair, that might have been caused partly by my reputation for proposing legislation that some considered arbitrary, if not draconian. There had been some quibbling, I realize, about my proposal that, by federal law, anybody caught selling macrame in public be dyed a natural shade and hung out to dry. That was also true about the law I proposed, as a registered representative of the Traveling People lobby, mandating that any city failing to provide clear and plentiful directional signs to the airport would lose its major league franchise.

There is, however, nothing remotely draconian about my property-tax proposal. It is thoroughly consistent with the American concepts of democratic decision making and local control. A City Council controlled by the aesthetes could exercise its mandate by assessing inert mobile homes or front-lawn flamingos at 800 percent of market value. If the philistines regained control at the next election, they could tax architectural understatement to their hearts' content. When the populists take over in Beverly Hills, they could double the tax rate for any house that included a private screening room.

Once the Malibu City Council also fell to the populists, left-wing producers who had always stretched chain-link fences between their $400,000 beach houses in order to keep the riffraff off the beach would find it to their economic advantage to change their views about who owns the shoreline. Accountants who might now phone a Malibu client to tell him that he has been taken out of oil drilling and into shrimp fishing will become accustomed to adding something like, "We're taking you out of No Trespassing and into Public Access and writing forty grand off the assessment the first year.'' The PRIVATE—NO TRES-PASSING signs would come down, to be replaced by signs saying PUBLIC BEACH—ALL WELCOME—HAVE A REAL NICE DAY—PLEASE STOP BY IF THE KIDS NEED TO USE THE BATHROOM.

For years, I have had a fantasy that helps me fall asleep peacefully: On some cold winter night, a paramilitary strike force of Townies in some place like Nantucket or Edgartown, Martha's Vineyard, ties up all watchmen thought to be loyal to the summer people and then paints every weathered shingle house in town, alternating house by house between turquoise and salmon pink. If property taxes were properly used, there would be no need for such turmoil. The Townies, safely in control of government all winter, would simply assess property owners $14 for each unpainted shingle, and then sit back while every house in town was painted by what one of my predecessors in this line of work referred to as the Invisible Hand. For the sake of such a peaceful transition, I'd even be willing to give up my fantasy about the strike force. I still have the one about the populists taking over in Beverly Hills.

It-all-goes-back-to-ism

November 1, 1978

When a bill was passed this summer requiring New York dog-walkers to clean up after their dogs, I was among those who said that the dog people could be expected to observe the new law at about the same pace that newspaper reporters and traveling salesmen observed the Volstead Act. "Dog people are anarchists," I said to my wife, Alice, "but not the interesting kind."

"That's a very unfair thing to say," Alice said.

"If you think that was unfair, listen to this," I said. "Dog people hate children. Otherwise, they would not allow their dogs to foul the footpaths where innocent little tots frolic and play stickball and pass smart-aleck remarks about grown-ups." I reminded Alice that Robert Bingham, a friend of ours who owns a Newfoundland, once told me that our daughters were merely "dog substitutes."

"Caleb Cooks has a dog," Alice said.

"So?"

"How can you say he hates children? He's a child."

Caleb Cooks is the little boy who lives downstairs. We go way back. "I always except my friends from my prejudices, Alice," I said. "You know that."

We happened to be out of the country for the entire summer, giving me some time to wonder whether I would have the courage to place the first law-defying dog-person I saw under citizen's arrest. I simply didn't know whether I would be able to approach someone who was holding the leash of a misbehaving (and perhaps mean-tempered and maybe even rabid) cocker spaniel and say, "On behalf of the citizens of the State of New York—Hugh L. Carey, Governor; Louis J. Lefkowitz, Attorney General—I place you under arrest for permitting an animal to foul the footpath. You have a right to counsel. You may remain silent. You may not giggle."

No such confrontation was necessary. We arrived back in New York to find that the dog-walkers on our street were scrupulously obeying the law. I was filled with remorse—a substance with which I am rarely filled. I believe I would have rushed up to the first dog-person I saw obeying the law to shake his hand and ask his forgiveness and congratulate him on his good citizenship—except that, as it happened, the first dog-person I saw obeying the law had both hands occupied, one with a leash and another with a strategically rolled copy of *The Wall Street Journal*. It occurred to me at the time that as a minor side-benefit of the new law, anyone wishing to describe the ephemeral nature of newspaper writing has another phrase to alternate with the old saw "Today's newspaper is tomorrow's fish wrapping."

Unfortunately, before we had been back a week, I ran into an it-all-goes-back-to-ist of my acquaintance. He solemnly informed me that New York's dramatic comeback in public esteem, a phenomenon then much discussed, could be traced to the willingness of the dog people to obey the law—a symbol of the city's spirit reborn. It-all-goes-back-to-ists explain anything by saying that it all goes back to something else—preferably something unlikely enough to have escaped the notice of other it-all-goes-back-to-ists. There are it-all-goes-back-to-ists, for instance, who believe that the disintegration of this country all goes back to the interstate highway system, and there are it-all-goes-back-to-ists who now say that Richard M. Nixon's downfall was inevitable from the moment he tried dressing the White House guards in the costumes of Ruritanian comic opera.

I naturally resented the intrusion of it-all-goes-back-to-ist theory into my new warm relationships with the dog people. "I don't mind shaking a dog-person's hand or patting one on the back or passing on a simple 'well done.' " I told Alice. "But I don't think I'm ready to thank them for the salvation of our culture. That much remorse I do not have." As it happens, I have always tried to avoid the temptations of it-all-goes-back-to-ism—although once, in a moment of weakness, I did say in public print that if the crumbling of the society went back to anything it goes back to agribusiness's vertical integration of the broiler industry.

I soon discovered that the comeback of New York was a subject it-all-goes-back-to-ists found irresistible. There is a school of thought that traces everything to the joyous spectacle of the Tall Ships in 1976, and there is a school that believes the city was saved by the Italian Communist Party (on the theory that the possibility of the Reds coming to power drove a lot of Milanese businessmen into the Manhattan real estate market). A number of specialists believe that it all goes back to seeing the back of Johnny Carson. The theory that New York was saved by Carson's departure for the West Coast leans heavily on a Syracuse University Graduate School of Communication Arts doctoral dissertation which shows that 83% of the jokes in Carson's opening monologue are about not getting a laugh on the previous joke, and that 78% of the remainder used to be about getting mugged in Central Park.

"I refuse to discuss the possibility that it all goes back to the dog people," I said to Alice one day.

"You may be right," she said. "A lot of people are now saying that it may all go back to Studio 54." The Studio 54 theory is based on the belief that the wretched sight of crowds trying to push into that *People* magazine version of purgatory made everyone in the rest of the country feel so left out that New York went way up in their esteem. I was silent for a moment.

"What do you think of the Studio 54 theory?" Alice said.

"I think it may be the first sensible argument I have ever heard for moving to Larchmont," I said, getting out of my chair.

"Where are you going?" Alice said.

"I'm going downstairs to thank Caleb for saving the city."

Exercising the Franchise

November 25, 1978

Early in the campaign for Governor of New York, I eliminated Perry Duryea from consideration after I saw him on a television program referring to himself in the third person. I never vote for a politician who refers to himself in the third person. It's a firm rule. As far as I'm concerned, the only public figure who ever got away with referring to himself in the third person was Satchel Paige, the philosopher king of several pitching staffs, and Ole' Satch, as he sometimes called himself, had the grace not to run for elective office.

Scratching Duryea left me without a candidate. I had long before decided that I could never vote for Hugh Carey, a man who hangs out in P.J. Clarke's with one of the Ford girls. My mother told me not to hang out in bars because the sort of people I would meet there were the sort of people who hang out in bars. As I remember it, the establishment she had in mind was LeRoy's Waldo Bar, in Kansas City, where I misspent part of my youth drinking Schlitz and talking dirty, but the rule certainly holds for P.J. Clarke's. In fact, if Kansas City had offered the range of saloons available in New York, I know my mother would have amended her rule by saying, "If you must hang out in bars, at least don't hang out in a bar that serves gossip columnists."

I have nothing personal against either of the Ford girls. (As a matter of policy, I have never distinguished between them, on the theory that, like the Ford Fairmont and the Mercury Zephyr, they may be essentially the same product with different names and a slight variation on the grill.) Anyone concerned with the economic well-being of American cities can hardly be critical of two people who through their debutante parties alone pumped $500,000 into the economy of Detroit. Still, it was, I believe, Dr. Johnson who said, "Sir, show me the escort of the deb of the year and I'll show you a creep." As many scholars have pointed out, Dr. Johnson was, some years ago, seen in the company of Brenda Fraser once or twice himself, but I see no reason to doubt his story that he was present only to treat her bronchitis.

People are always telling me that I should vote on the issues. Someone who votes on the issues, I suppose, would have cast his ballot for Kennedy over Nixon in 1960 on the basis of preferring Kennedy's position on some constantly discussed campaign issue like the defense of Quemoy and Matsu. Only at the risk of being dismissed as frivolous could people vote for Kennedy rather than Nixon on the simple ground that any man who delivered the Checkers speech without giggling was a certifiable wonk, registered and with papers. As it turned out, of course, the issue of defending Quemoy and Matsu was less important to the survival of the Republic than wonkiness.

I did try voting on the issues for a while, but it didn't

work. Having pored over the opposing position papers, I would cast my ballot as an informed citizen—and the country would continue to be run by fools and thieves and even an occasional poltroon. Finally, I got smart. If voting on the issues was doing the country no good at all, I figured, I might as well have the pleasure of treating political candidates as applicants for a club that had a single opening and maintained an admissions committee of one—me. I can't claim that the new method has caused any improvement in the quality of our political leadership, but it has saved me a lot of dreary research on the history of Quemoy and Matsu.

Some years ago, when the neighborhood where Little Italy meets Chinatown was still overwhelmingly Italian, a Chinese candidate for the New York Assembly breezed into my club simply by saying that he was running even though he didn't have "a Chinaman's chance." My favorite gubernatorial candidate in recent years was John Alsop, an insurance executive from Hartford who ran for Governor in Connecticut on the Republican ticket. Alsop is a brother of the Washington columnists, and used to be known among the mean-spirited in Connecticut as "the smart Alsop." Challenged outside the factory gate by a sarcastic worker who said, "I bet you're for motherhood and apple pie and the flag," Alsop replied, "That's absolutely correct. And I stand opposed to man-eating sharks." Only the residency requirements prevented me from voting for Alsop or for the pessimistic Chinese Assembly candidate or for an ape from the Atlanta zoo named Willie B., who was once run in a Congressional race against an incumbent of Pleistocene political thought and attracted the motto "Vote for Willie B.—Let Us Begin Again."

Reading about Susan Ford filming a Subaru commercial in front of the White House or Billy Carter opening yet another shopping center, I wrestle with the question of whether or not I can hold a candidate's family against him. Is that the sort of club I'm running? I do have what I believe the lawyers might call a benign precedent for taking family into consideration. When John Lindsay defeated first the diminutive Mario Procaccino and then Abe Beame, the vest-pocket city comptroller, the victories were generally explained by the fact that most New York voters, descendants of one or another sort of stunted immigrants themselves, were under the impression that the tall and handsome Lindsay was what authentic Americans were supposed to look like. The most succinct analysis of Lindsay's two mayoral victories was made by a long-time commentator on city politics named Doug Ireland: "Big Deal! He only beat ten foot six altogether." My support of Lindsay, though, had nothing to do with his appearance. It was based on the report that his wife had reacted to being stashed in the ladies' balcony at the annual Inner Circle political dinner by quietly flicking peanuts on the diners below. At our club, after all, new members are encouraged to bring their spouses to Happy Hour, and it was comforting to have the assurance that at least one new member would bring someone who knows how to behave in any situation.

The Truth Will Out

December 16, 1978

As a lover of truth, I am naturally pleased to see the facts emerging about the prediction attributed to H. L. Mencken concerning the first President from the Deep South. It is gratifying to see yet another confirmation of that old American political adage, usually credited to the late John Foster Dulles: "You can't fool all of the people all of the time, but you might as well give it your best shot."

I suppose what stirred interest in the passage from the start was that, by chance, the First Family Mencken envisioned seemed rather close to our very own First Family—a beer-swilling brother, a cousin on the Hallelujah circuit, a daughter taking pictures with her box camera, and an incumbent who, "shorn of his bumpkin ways by some of Grady's New South hucksters, will have a charm comparable to that of the leading undertaker of Dothan, Alabama." Last spring, I reprinted the Mencken quotation in this column—reprinted it routinely, I might add, in the way that American newspapers once routinely reprinted the body count handed out each day by the U.S. Army spokesman in Saigon.

For a while, other publications reprinted the passage as routinely as I had. Then we were faced with what I can only call a backlash. It was led by Georgia state Senator Julian Bond, whose statesmanlike exterior, I know, has masked a deep sense of frustration and rage ever since he managed, in 1961, to integrate the public tennis courts of Atlanta only to be beaten in straight sets by a female dietitian in her late 50s. Bond himself reprinted the Mencken passage in a column for the Atlanta *Gazette,* provoking a *Los Angeles Times* investigation of its origin which has not been matched for journalistic enterprise since my own investigation, in the early 1970s, uncovered a conspiracy between Richard M. Nixon and Willard Marriott to consolidate all of the cooking in this country into one gigantic kitchen, to be located somewhere in Virginia.

The *Los Angeles Times* reporter, Jeff Prugh, questioned a number of Mencken scholars, including Alistair Cooke, who put together *The Vintage Mencken* long before he met the Bellamys. According to Prugh's account, Cooke "pored voraciously" over his Mencken collection for nine days, and then concluded that the passage was a "mischievous parody." The tip-off, Cooke said, was the use of the word "pornographer," as in the President's cousin "praying for the conversion of some Northern Sodom's most Satanic pornographer as she waves his work—well thumbed—for all the yokels to gasp at." Informing Prugh that "pornographer" was little used in the 1920s, Cooke offered the opinion that the entire passage may have been invented by Julian Bond.

A few days later, Bond hastened to clear himself by telling the implacable Prugh that the passage may have originated in this column. I had to face up to the implication carried in Bond's words: there was a possibility that the person who passed the quotation on to me, a person I have refused to say was or was not Zbigniew Brzezinski, had taken advantage of my trusting nature. But Bond, like one of those fallen-away Stalinists who immediately start accusing everyone of being an agent of the Red Menace, began writing letters to the editor claiming that I was not what the committee used to dismiss as an "innocent dupe" but the inventor of the quotation myself—a conscious hoaxer of the American people who had been caught at last by the wily Cooke. According to Bond's letters, I had been driven to the deed by my embarrassment at having been snookered many years before by "a story about 'seal boy,' a youth who fell off a boat in the Gulf of Mexico and was raised by porpoises." I was not so much angry as a little bit hurt.

Even that was not the unkindest cut. In writing a review of a book I recently published, my own wife, in the very magazine that publishes this column, implied that I had invented the Mencken quotation—a charge made in direct violation of the rule of evidence that prohibits a wife from testifying against her husband in a journal of opinion. The state of mind my wife was in when she tossed off this calumny can best be described by noting that her review of my book was distinctly unfavorable.

Then, as so often happens in America these days, the truth began to emerge through the efforts of an accountant. Don Harvey, an accountant in Chicago, wrote me to say that "pornographer" was not only used in the '20s but had been used by Mencken himself in 1920 in a *New Republic* article called "Star Spangled Men." If I did not have access to back numbers of *The New Republic,* Harvey said,

I could find the same essay reprinted in *The Vintage Mencken,* collected and with an introduction by Alistair Cooke.

This raises a number of questions about Cooke's role. If the Mencken quote is not genuine, why did Cooke try to shift the blame to Julian Bond? Does Cooke know Brzezinski? Does he know Don Harvey? Is it possible that Cooke had something to do with making up the quote and now fears he may be deported if discovered? Is Alistair Cooke an American citizen? If so, why does he talk so funny?

Once the truth began to emerge, it overwhelmed the naysayers and cynics. Only last month, in the course of interviewing a visiting specialist on the subject (me), the Kansas City *Star* finally printed the truth about the seal boy hoax. "The Seal Boy Hoax (a boy who supposedly lived with dolphins in the Gulf of Mexico) was a confusion Bond took for real," the *Star* article said. "He reported it, and then blamed Trillin when the truth was made known."

Recently, I received a letter about the Mencken quotation from John Givens, the news director of WAGF in Dothan, Alabama. "I could dismiss the quote as being a hoax," Mr. Givens wrote, "Instead of that, I asked around town and found that the piece reeks of Mencken's pen and may very well be authentic. Let me explain that H. L. Mencken was very much familiar with Dothan, Alabama . . ." After listing some of Mencken's Dothan connections and reaffirming his own belief in the quotation, Mr. Givens ends by saying, "I would appreciate some insight to its authenticity." This, Mr. Givens, is it.

Losing China

January 6, 1979

"Daddy, I don't understand what it means that we've finally recognized China. Was it wearing a disguise or something?"

"Yes. For twenty-five years, China pretended to be the Republic of Rwanda. Naturally, we had no idea who it really was, although the disguise was much too small for it, and China bulged out all over, sometimes into Tibet or North Korea. We knew it wasn't the Republic of Rwanda, of course, because there already was a Republic of Rwanda in Africa. Also, no Chinese diplomat could pronounce the Republic of Rwanda."

"Mommy says she can never get a straight answer out of you either."

"Well, diplomatic recognition is a very complicated question. Why don't you ever ask me the kind of questions other little girls ask their fathers? The capital of North Dakota, how to spell 'disgusting'—that sort of thing."

"What *is* the capital of North Dakota?"

"That's a very complicated question. Do you want more Cheerios?"

"Didn't I hear you talking to Uncle Bill about the time we lost China?"

"I'm pleased that you happened to hear one of our foreign policy discussions. Your mother would have people believe that Uncle Bill and I talk about nothing but sex and violence and exotic flavors of ice cream.''

''If China's so big, how could we lose it?''

''We didn't lose it that way. We lost it the way Uncle Bill sometimes says that he had the Giants and ten points, and lost his shirt.''

''Lost it to who?''

''Whom, not who. I may not know much about foreign policy, but I'm a whiz on grammar. Your question should have been 'Uncle Bill lost his shirt to whom?' ''

''Not Uncle Bill's shirt, daddy. China. To whom did we lose China?''

''I always had trouble with that one myself. Maybe you could ask your mother.''

''If we lost it, we must have had it.''

''Well, we had what Uncle Bill would call a piece of the action. Then there was a civil war, and the people we didn't like because they were Communists beat the people we had a piece of, so our people had to take over somebody else's island and call that China.''

''You mean there was an island disguised as China?''

''Exactly. The disguise was too big for the island, of course, and we had to keep stuffing it with foreign aid to make it fit.''

''I think I understand to whom China was lost, but whom lost it?''

''Who lost it. Not whom. Who.''

''Please don't start talking about Uncle Bill's shirt again, daddy. It just mixes me up.''

''Your Uncle Bill had nothing to do with losing China.

I'll admit that he may do some fiddling with the laws governing New York State Sales Tax now and then, but basically your Uncle Bill is a loyal citizen."

"Then who lost it?"

"Well, fortunately, there were a lot of hearings and investigations at the time, and it was decided that China was lost by the people who were right about which side was going to win the war. To use a very simple analogy, it's as if Uncle Bill's bookie predicted that the Giants would lose, then the Giants do lose, so the people who bet on the Giants have the bookie jailed for breaking and entering."

"I hate your analogies, daddy. Just tell me in a regular way: Are the people who lost China the same people who won it back?"

"Oh no. The people who lost China lost their jobs for losing China and had to live in disgrace the entire time that China was disguised as the Republic of Rwanda."

"Then please just give me a straight answer: Who won it back?"

"Richard M. Nixon won it back."

"Richard M. Nixon!"

"See how boring straight answers are?"

"And he wasn't one of the people who lost it in the first place?"

"Certainly not. In fact, he called the other people traitors for losing it, and he insisted for twenty years that only traitors would point out that the disguise of the island we had disguised as China was getting baggy around the knees. Are you sure you wouldn't rather talk about sex and violence and exotic flavors of ice cream?"

"I think I understand. If recognizing China twenty years

ago was losing it and recognizing it now is winning it, the people we didn't like there must have become a lot nicer, so now we like them. What have they done since we lost them?"

"Well, they killed a lot of our soldiers in Korea and they called us running dogs of capitalism. Also imperialistic lackeys."

"Then why do we think they're so nice now?"

"Because they also called the Russians running dogs of capitalism. The way our foreign policy works, it's O.K. to kill people and call people rude names as long as you don't like the Russians, because the Russians are Communists."

"But I thought you said the Chinese were Communists, and that's why we didn't recognize them."

"Are you sure you don't want any more Cheerios? They're stinky with riboflavin."

"Really, daddy."

"Pierre."

"Pierre's a Communist? Pierre whom? I mean Pierre who?"

"Pierre is the capital of North Dakota."

"Daddy, Pierre is the capital of *South* Dakota, you dumdum."

"Well, it's a very complicated question."

Iran for Christmas

February 3, 1979

For Christmas, I took over Iran for Alice. I don't mean I went there with a band of mercenaries, recruited from the better Manhattan saloons, took over the government, and presented Alice with all of the rights and privileges accruing to the Peacock Throne. I try to avoid travel during the holiday season. What I mean is that I took over keeping up with what was happening in Iran, giving Alice a little extra time to devote to the Middle East peace talks and the January sales.

On Christmas, there was a moment when I feared that I had not chosen well. As I watched her open the package containing Iran—I had wrapped it in some rather colorful paper whose print, it seemed to me, suggested a Persian rug if viewed in that spirit—I thought I saw the flicker of a frown on her face. "She was hoping for the SALT talks," I said to myself.

I had thought about getting her SALT instead of Iran. I knew she despised protracted negotiations. Once, having heard on a talk show that presenting surprise gifts for no particular occasion was one secret of keeping the romance in a marriage, I had returned from the office on a rainy, uneventful Tuesday and announced to Alice that she need no longer concern herself with a British coal strike then in its third week. She was ecstatic. SALT, I realized, was a drearier subject than Iran—lacking even the stimulation of a story now and then about some particularly revolting act of conspicuous consumption by the Shah and his family. But the papers had not been carrying much about the SALT talks, and there were thousands of words daily to read about Iran. Somehow, SALT had seemed a smaller gift.

"Actually, I thought about getting you the SALT talks," I said tentatively.

"Oh, no. This is much nicer," Alice said. "It was just that the wrapping seemed a little tacky."

"You said a few weeks ago that you hated worrying about how to pronounce Ayatullah Khomeini. Was that a hint?"

"Well, it's certainly true anyway," Alice said. "Also, plowing through those oil production figures was a bore, and all of those endless speculations about whether or not 'American intelligence was caught napping' just made me sleepy. This is perfect. Really. I love it. Just think of not having to concern myself anymore about knowing whether the Shah is about to leave and where he might go! I was beginning to feel like a travel agent."

"Probably the United States, although Gstaad has also been mentioned by informed observers in Teheran," I said.

"What?"

"I was just telling you what's in the paper this morning," I said. "The gift has begun."

Alice started it all some years ago by giving me Cyprus for my birthday. I was delighted—and only partly because I had somehow got it into my head that she was planning to give me an orange vinyl tie. For some years, I had been thinking that the task of being a well-informed citizen was particularly onerous when it came to Cyprus. On the Cyprus question, I craved ignorance. I was tired of the Bishop. The history of Greek and Turkish settlement failed to fascinate. Any analysis of the effect a Greek-Turkish conflict might have on NATO caused me to long for the Arts & Leisure Section.

Sometimes, Cyprus seemed to disappear from the papers for years, only to surface in an even more desperate crisis, full of pathetic refugees and ponderous United Nations debates. Cyprus had begun to remind me of some dreadful old uncle who is always alarming the family with emergencies that are invariably described as beyond solution: Something must be done immediately before Uncle Harry's behavior drives Aunt Thelma to violence. How long can a man continue to shoot at postmen with a crossbow before tragedy occurs? Can a fanatic Christian Scientist and a homicidal podiatrist live together for another day? Then, people in the family become distracted by their own problems, everyone forgets about Uncle Harry for months, and suddenly he re-emerges—with problems just as insoluble as ever. Who solved the insoluble emergencies in the meantime? Should citizens who already have Uncle Harrys be expected to worry about Cyprus as well?

"Don't Give It Another Thought," Alice's birthday gift to me had said, printed in colorful letters on a map of the dread island. "Leave It to Me."

"Could that really be?" I had asked incredulously. I was almost overcome with gratitude—not to mention a little guilt for having thought, even for a moment, that a woman who could think of such a gift might have stuck me with an orange vinyl necktie.

'You just tell me now at which point you care to be informed,'' Alice said. ''I can let you know when it appears that they're going to start fighting again, for instance, or I can let you know when it's getting to the point at which the NATO alliance might be seriously weakened.''

I thought about it for a while. ''Worldwide nuclear conflagration,'' I finally said. ''If it appears that because of Cyprus worldwide nuclear conflagration is imminent, I would appreciate being informed. If not, I'll just give it a skip, thank you very much.''

After all of those years of freedom from the wretched Cypriots, I found it gratifying, of course, to begin a Christmas Day by presenting Alice with a gift that would lift from her shoulders the daily strain of distinguishing between Gen. Gholam ali Oveissi and Gen. Manuchehr Khosrowdad. I was filled with Christmas warmth as I opened my own gift. It was a map. I recognized it immediately from my research: Iran. ''Don't Give It Another Thought,'' the printing on it said. ''Leave It to Me.''

Julian Bond Exposed

February 24, 1979

"The truth about the tennis court integration did involve a woman; no fifty-year-old she, but a tan, lissome lovely selected for the photos I knew would be taken of this historic step forward in race relations."

—Julian Bond, in a letter
The Nation *declined to publish.*

The truth about Julian Bond's integration of the Atlanta public tennis courts can now be told, although not by Julian Bond, whose memory is as undependable as his backhand. Information not available at the time indicates, for instance, that the original plan was to integrate the Atlanta public golf course—a plan that was vetoed by the directors of the Student Non-Violent Coordinating Committee on the ground that, considering the severity of Bond's slice, no golf course demonstration he took part in could be assured of being considered completely nonviolent.

Although Atlanta was, in 1961, already building a national reputation as "the city too busy to hate"—a motto that a few local cynics translated as Babbittry Over Bigotry—it was almost completely segregated. A boycott by black people of all Atlanta department stores was energized by weekly mass meetings in which ministers of the A. M. E. Church, all competing in the Martin Luther King Jr. Extended Metaphor Contest, described how black people everywhere would emerge from the long, dark night of segregation into the bright new dawn of emancipation.

Except for King, most of those whose names associated Atlanta with the leadership of the national civil rights movement were not on the scene. Vernon Jordan was still in law school at DePauw. Andrew Young had not joined King's staff. Jimmy Carter was a member of the Sumter County School Board, which had vowed to shut down every school in the county rather than admit one black student—a position Carter supporters later defended by pointing out that Sumter County happened to be in a section of Georgia where closing the schools would have no appreciable effect on the educational attainments of the populace.

Carl Holman, who was later to become executive director of the Urban Coalition, did happen to be in Atlanta at the time, teaching at Clark College and presiding over a lively weekly newspaper called *The Atlanta Inquirer*. The *Inquirer*'s staff consisted of black students involved in the Atlanta sit-in movement, including a quiet young man named Julian Bond. A member of a family long prominent in black education, Bond had just returned to Atlanta from prep school in the East—a source of some not-so-gentle joshing from tough young sit-in veterans, who liked to ask him about sit-ins at tea dances and the hardship facing anyone determined to integrate the chess club.

Resolutely, Bond set out to win his reputation in the movement. After his plan for golf course integration had been rejected, he resolved to integrate the public tennis courts. It is ironic that Bond now refers to this demonstration as a "step forward," since that is precisely the term that had been used in Eastern prep school circles to describe his serve. Bond did indeed ask a "tan, lissome lovely" to play on the historic day—one Melissa Mae Brumble—but, being a graduate of Emma Willard herself, she knew that Bond's prep school nickname had been "Foot Fault" Bond. Under advice of counsel, she refused to play him.

Desperate for a partner, Bond turned to Edna Scroggins, a mildly eccentric but fearlessly liberal member of an Atlanta white family that had made a fortune in soy waste. Bond's objection to a reference to the match that appeared in this column recently (". . . Julian Bond, whose statesmanlike exterior, I know, has masked a keen sense of frustration and rage ever since he managed, in 1961, to integrate the public tennis courts of Atlanta only to be beaten in straight sets by a female dietitian in her late fifties") was apparently based on a belief that the description of Mrs. Scroggins made her sound like an unimposing opponent. In Atlanta tennis circles, though, Mrs. Scroggins—who was indeed a female dietitian in her late fifties—was considered to have made great strides in overcoming the disadvantages of her age and her obesity and a rather severe case of the gout. As it happened, no photos were taken, but *The Atlanta Constitution* carried a summary of the match by the husband of Edna Scroggins: "Edna's a nice old bag of bones who just happens to have a better backhand than that little colored fella."

Our Family Slogan

March 17, 1979

Oddly enough, the slogan that President Carter tried to plant in the public mind through his State of the Union Message—a New Foundation—was rejected as a slogan for our family several months ago. We decided against it because of our concern that it would only make me worry about the foundation of our house. As far as I know, there is nothing at all wrong with the foundation of our house, but I happen to come from a long line of people whose minds have tended to dwell morbidly on underpinnings. Among my forebears, simply mentioning the word "foundation" has always conjured up horrifying images of cracks opening in the basement walls or ferocious insects gnawing away at the sills. I had a cousin who was convinced that his house was built on the San Adreas Fault even though he lived in St. Joseph, Missouri. When somebody says New Foundation to me, I do not think of the American people building new foundations for a stable and just society. I think of a contractor—a sullen, beady-eyed contractor—saying, "I'm afraid what you're going to need here, my friend, is a new foundation."

All of which left us without a slogan for the family. For years, I had assumed that we could do without a family slogan, but then the Mohlers, down the street, started calling themselves the Great Society.

"I just don't see how a fat lady and a man who is practically under indictment for tax evasion can go around calling themselves the Great Society," my wife, Alice, said.

"Well, they do," I said. "Right on their stationery it says 'Harry and Greta Mohler—The Great Society.' Everybody seems to be doing it. The Palermos have a sign on their mailbox that says 'The Palermos—First Family of Chestnut Street,' and that horde of Clanceys up the street now answer the phone by saying 'Big and Small, We Got 'Em All.' "

"I don't think we need a slogan," Alice said. "Slogans are tacky."

"You promised," our daughter Abigail said. Abigail, who is 10, is the Amnesty International representative assigned to keep our family free of injustice, torture, confinement on political grounds and assorted atrocities. She seems sweet, but she is a killer at the negotiating table. It was Abigail who hammered out an agreement acceptable to both sides after her younger sister, Sarah, refused to take a nap until American troops withdrew from Southeast Asia.

"When I was a child, my family had no slogan," I said. "Unless you want to count 'Zip Up Your Jacket.' Kids nowadays expect too much."

"I hope you're not going to start one of those stories about how you had to walk twelve miles to school," Abigail said.

"Grandma told us it was only about six blocks and you

made her drive you there if it was the teeniest bit cold,'' Sarah said.

''And what would she say when I got out of the car?''

''Zip Up Your Jacket,'' Abigail and Sarah said, in unison.

''Still a very serviceable slogan,'' I said. ''We could get many more years of use out of it.''

''It's a yucky slogan,'' Abigail said.

''I hate it,'' Sarah said.

I was about to begin a speech about how children whose father walked twelve miles to school couldn't expect to have a new slogan every year, but then Alice said that the Bowens, across the street, already had ''Zip Up Your Jacket'' inscribed on the side of their Dodge Dart.

I thought about using the New Deal for a while, although we don't really have a new deal in our family. It's the same old deal. Also, someone who worked in the New Deal is almost never referred to these days except as ''an old New Dealer''—a description I thought Alice might consider more appropriate to Greta Mohler than to herself. The other slogans used by Presidential Administrations seemed difficult to apply to people rather than programs. What, in fact, will Hamilton Jordan and Jody Powell and Bert Lance and this Administration's other contributions to statecraft be called in their dotage? Old New Foundationists? Old New Foundationites? If Leonard Garment, Nixon's counsel, had stayed on under Carter—and, as things have turned out, he might well have—he could at least be called an old New Foundation Garment, but he has, as they say, gone back to the law. How would those who toiled for Lyndon Johnson refer to each other in reunions to come? Old Great Societyators?

The pressure was building in our house. The Bernsteins, whose daughter was in school with Abigail, had taken to listing themselves in the telephone book as "The Best Mixed Marriage Yet."

"It's not fair," Abigail said. "Everyone at school has a slogan except us. Samantha's family now has bumper stickers that say 'The Bartletts—A Triumph of Group Therapy.' "

"How about 'A Chicken in Every Pot, Two Cars in Every Garage?' " I said.

"I hate chicken," Sarah said. "Except for white meat."

"Well, how about 'An All-White-Meat Chicken in Every Pot?' "

"Also, the skin is yucky," Sarah said.

I was about to alter the slogan to rule out yucky skin when I saw Abigail put her jacket on and prepare to leave. The walkout has always been one of her favorite negotiating devices. "You're not making a serious offer," she said. "I'm going outside to play."

"Zip up your jacket," I said.

Card-Counters Count

April 28, 1979

Suspicions that I am, by the standards of *The Nation,* not well and truly committed to the cause of the oppressed, will surely be evaporated by the intensity with which I support Kenneth Uston, who was ejected from the Resorts International casino in Atlantic City for playing blackjack too well. I would sign petitions for Uston, perhaps even legibly. I would march in any demonstration for him—any demonstration, at least, that was held in a place reasonably convenient to my neighborhood and was organized in a way that assured protection from hooligans hired by the forces of reaction. If Uston were in need of financial aid, I would throw my home open for a cocktail party to benefit his legal defense fund—a statement I make knowing full well that the A.C.L.U. is bearing the costs of his litigation and that Uston himself won $43,000 in Atlantic City before Resorts International wised up and showed him the door. I support Kenneth Uston, in other words, without qualification.

I take this stand, I might add, without having anything to gain personally from seeing justice triumph in Uston's case. This is not like those intellectuals supporting Larry Flynt on the proposition that once the prosecuting attorney of Fulton County has whetted his teeth on *Hustler* he will inevitably turn his attention to lyric poetry or essays comparing Christopher Marlowe to the early films of Wallace Beery. Uston is what is known as a card-counter: He reduces the house odds in blackjack by remembering how many face cards have been played and betting accordingly. I am not a card-counter. I think I can say, without intending any disrespect to the oppressed Uston, that I don't even particularly like card-counters. I rank them with diet-balancers and budget-makers and trim-and-gutter-maintainers as people who seem to take pleasure in behaving in ways that remind me of what I would be doing if I were a person of somewhat better character. One reason I never took up bridge is that I knew I would resent the people who kept track of the cards that had been played while I allowed my attention to wander in the direction of speculations on what the hostess might be planning by way of an after-game snack.

Another reason I never took up bridge is the knowledge that even if I counted the cards I could never remember the count. I have difficulty remembering anything—an affliction I trace to having had to memorize the Greek alphabet, forward and backward, for admission to a high school club. It has become obvious to me that knowing the Greek alphabet leaves practically no room in my memory for anything else. (I do not subscribe to the theory that only a small portion of our gray matter is actually used; I am convinced that all of us are operating at full throttle.) For years, I've been trying to forget the Greek alphabet. Some time ago, I finally managed to forget it backward—an achievement that was presumably responsible for my being able, at last, to commit my Army serial number to memory, years after my discharge—but I still can't seem to forget it forward. Uston claims he can teach anybody to be a card-counter, but he couldn't teach me—at least not while my mind remains cluttered with useless letters of foreign origin.

My support of Uston, then, is based on no bias in his favor but simply on the belief that he is being penalized for doing what all Americans are constantly exhorted to do—learning to play the game better than anyone else plays it. Nobody has accused him of using trick decks or concealed mirrors. He has not been charged with bribing barmaids to corrupt dealers. He stands accused of skill in his chosen game. It's as if high school outfielders, propelled through the agonies of training by dreams of major league contracts and shaving cream endorsements, were told by the coach, "Don't learn to play *too* well, though, or you might be asked to leave. Upsets the other fellows, you know."

If Resorts International had been acting on its own, I think I could remain calm—all of us supporters of the oppressed having grown accustomed to acts of greed and even piracy by corporations. But the casino management was acting under the explicit authorization of the New Jersey Casino Control Commission. According to *The New York Times,* the commission chairman explained that "he felt that casinos here must be profitable or other casino companies would not seek licenses, which would cut state taxes and halt the economic revival of Atlantic City." The state, in other words, has a stake in seeing to it that its citizens are systematically relieved of their paychecks by a gambling casino. A plumber from Bayonne who comes out ahead after a day at the blackjack table may have a warm glow on for a while, but he has acted contrary to the public policy of the state of New Jersey. He would, I suppose, be guilty of undermining his state even further by driving home at a lawful speed—depriving New Jersey of needed revenue it might obtain from a speeding fine.

The state gave Resorts International permission to post a sign near the gaming tables that says WE RESERVE THE RIGHT TO EXCLUDE PROFESSIONAL CARD-COUNTERS FROM PLAY AT OUR BLACKJACK TABLES. The word "professional" is obviously meant to carry with it some justification for the ban: The other folks are welcome because they're just having a good time. The owners of Resorts International are having a particularly good time; in their effort to help the state along financially, they expect to take a quarter of a billion dollars off the suckers this year. With that kind of money, they should be able to hire a sign-writer who does not suffer from prolixity. The sign banning card-counters should say simply LOSERS ONLY. If the state needs further financial support, Resorts International could post another sign at the door that says TAKE A CHANCE ON THE TURNPIKE—DON'T BE A SISSY.

that Kopkind, normally an even-tempered person, flew into a rage late in the evening when the members of a mariachi band insisted that the number he had requested, "Indian Love Call," was truly not in their repertoire.

As it happens, I had at first been all for sending in Kopkind's record to *Guinness.* I figured I owed the *Guinness Book of World Records* a favor. In the late 1950s, I had found myself in the London bureau of Time Inc., where, having so little experience in the organization that I had not yet even learned how to invert sentences, I was assigned the queries from New York that were considered the most bizarre or frivolous. One week, I was handed one saying that *Fortune* magazine needed to know at once—or "soonest," as the researchers who wrote the cables always said, since they spoke only a sort of pidgin cable-ese—which street in London was the longest street uninterrupted by intersections. There was no indication of just why *Fortune* magazine needed that information soonest. For a while, I tried to imagine the sentence of a *Fortune* story such a fact might fit into ("Sophisticated Londoners have always known, in the way they know that the longest street in London uninterrupted by intersections is Something Street, that the most powerful figure in the Bank of England is the daft but wily Lord Boodle of Gelt"), but the bureau's Old Hand had warned me that such imaginings brought on only acid-stomach and a poor attitude toward one's work. The way to proceed, I knew, was simply to find the fact that was needed and send it to New York soonest, as if the publisher was saying to the directors of the company, gathered in emergency session, "I think I'd have a good shot at keeping this whole operation from going under, gentlemen, if only I knew what street in London was the longest street uninterrupted by intersections.''

I couldn't find it. I called the traffic department. I called the street department. I called the sanitation department. The fact I needed soonest, it turned out, was not a fact that anyone had any cause to know.

''Call the McWhirters,'' the Old Hand told me. This was only a couple of years after Norris McWhirter and his brother, Ross, had begun publishing the *Guinness Book of World Records*—long before the book attained the sort of popularity that sent undergraduates into frenzies of marathon Ping-Pong playing or giant doughnut baking. I had never heard of the McWhirters.

I can't remember which of the brothers answered, but I remember precisely what his first question was after I had presented my problem: ''Do tunnels count?'' I realized that the Old Hand had steered me right once again. I thought it over for a while. I was in London. The researcher who had sent the query was 3,000 miles away—as far from being able to check my fact as I was from being able to divine her interest in it. ''Tunnels count,'' I finally said. I was told the name of the longest street in London uninterrupted by intersections. The magazine was saved.

In Ensenada, my obvious instinct was to return the favor, and, the morning after Kopkind's feat, I suggested to him that we cable London immediately. He was against it. I was surprised, although it is true that he was not in the best mood I had ever seen him in. ''But why?'' I said.

''In the first place,'' he said, ''I had only six margaritas.''

''Let us not quibble, Kopkind,'' I said. I was about to leave for the cable office when Kopkind gave me a better reason for remaining silent. He said that being in the *Guinness Book of World Records* for margarita drinking would be like having a reputation as the fastest gun in the West. The young margarita drinkers wanting to make a name for themselves would search him out. Even after years had passed, he wouldn't be able to walk into a bar for a solitary scotch without the possibility that some stranger would saunter up to him and say something like, ''I hear you think you can hold a lot of 'ritas, pops.'' Kopkind, I knew, was not the sort of person who could resist such challenges. He might end up pickled in tequila. I kept the world record to myself. Now, I'm glad I did. Norris McWhirter would probably make a special trip from London to say that, in the opinion of several renowned physiologists who were asked how many margaritas it would take for a man of normal height and weight to get to the point of asking a mariachi band to play ''Indian Love Call,'' Kopkind could have had only twenty-nine. Or six.

The Dark Side

June 16, 1979

Not long ago, I became preoccupied with the cost of the wristwatches worn by members of the New Jersey State Legislature. That sort of thing seems to come over me now and then. Once, ten or twelve years ago, I became intensely interested in just who was wearing Nehru jackets. I began making a list. I worked hard on the list—permitting my other responsibilities to slide, some said, and taking less care than I should about my personal appearance. I added new names as the evidence warranted. I deleted the names of people who had been included erroneously—perhaps because they had seemed to be wearing a Nehru jacket when they were actually wearing a Mao jacket. (I had a separate list for Mao jackets.) I still keep the Nehru-jacket list in my safety deposit box. Now and then, I take it out and read it slowly, savoring the names of prominent novelists and respectable government officials the way a stamp collector might savor his Mauritian special issues and Luxembourg misprints. Sometimes, I'll admit, I feel mean-spirited sitting alone in the corner of a safety deposit room at the Morgan Guaranty Trust Company, cackling over the names on my Nehru-jacket list. "This sort of thing is beneath you," I say to myself. Apparently it isn't.

I felt myself being drawn toward legislative timepieces a few months ago in Atlantic City, where I happened to be attending a hearing on housing conducted by the Legislature's oversight committee on casino gambling. I'm afraid my attention had been slipping away from the business at hand. Being of a sensitive disposition, I find it difficult to concentrate on more than two or three hours of testimony about impoverished Puerto Rican families being tossed out of their wretched apartments so that a real estate flipper can sell the land to a casino. My eyes began to wander. They passed, by chance, over the wristwatch being worn by the legislator who was conducting the hearing. I went back for a second look. What he was wearing on his wrist was not the sort of object I have in mind when I think of wristwatches. It was more in the range of a Cadillac Eldorado, or maybe a small nightclub. Its band was gold—obviously so supple that it could be used to tie a particularly grand gift package. Diamonds flashed from every corner of the face. The center of the face was a sleek black mystery—until the Assemblyman touched some secret button, at which time it became alive with digital reminders of the time and the date and other matters that I could only imagine. The winning numbers at Belmont? The temperature in Saint-Jean-Cap-Ferrat? The number of years over which various holdings can be depreciated under the latest tax law?

I found myself studying the watches of the other committee members. Cadillac Eldorados every one! Having observed what the social scientists call a fair sampling of the members of the Legislature, I realized that the Governor of New Jersey might have been able to avoid that unpopular state income tax if only, on the last day of some legislative session, he had been able to persuade the legislators to leave their watches on their desks before departing.

But why should I attach any sinister significance to that fact? Did I really believe that a man forfeits his right to wear the wristwatch of his choice when he takes the oath as a state legislator? Is it an Assemblyman's fault that Puerto Ricans persist in living in apartments that are worth less than his wristwatch? Why did I assume that a state legislator who was wearing a $200,000 wristwatch came by it through nefarious means? After all, he could be a man of independent wealth—gained, perhaps, from shrewd investments in Atlantic City real estate. Why was I so mean-spirited? Wasn't that sort of thing beneath me? Apparently it wasn't.

Taking pleasure in the dark side may be some sort of occupational hazard for reporters. Some years ago, while working on a piece about mailing lists, I was entertained by discovering that two of the most successful lists for selling *An ABZ of Love* were lists of psychiatrists and a list of graduates of the Harvard Business School. Finding that the best list for Republican fund raising was a list of people who had sent away for *Six Crises,* the kvetch classic, didn't interest me much. What I savored was the fact that a list almost as effective for the Republicans was a list of people who had sent away for Kozak, a cloth for cleaning cars without the use of water. That confirmed my suspicion of what a big Republican contributor might be like: a miserly old goat standing in front of his two-car garage, obsessed with preserving his expensive car but too stiff to get himself a little wet while doing it. (The big Democratic contributor, I figured, enjoyed getting himself soaked while washing a car that was equally expensive.) I was able to add a welcome detail to my picture of the fat cat when I discovered that one of the most effective lists for attracting subscribers to *Kiplinger's Newsletter,* a straight-poop Washington report that appealed to business executives, was a list of people who had sent away for Klipette, a device for removing nose hair.

"I have to quit thinking this way," I said to myself as the testimony droned on in Atlantic City. "Pretty soon, I'll be making lists of people who wore Nehru jackets and own multimillion-dollar watches and have a bulge in their pocket that looks suspiciously like a Klipette." Was I really the sort of person who judged a man by the way he dressed? Did I stand in favor of hairy noses? I finally managed to put the cost of the wristwatches of New Jersey legislators out of my mind. What worries me now is that one of those modern political scientists who finds truth in numbers is probably studying this very matter with a computer. He is adding up the value of the watches of the members of each State Legislature. He is dividing by the number of members. He is dividing that number by the number of indictments handed down against legislators in the previous year. He is producing a figure that confirms what I have known from the start.

Making a Scene

July 7, 1979

Foreign policy analysts disagree about the cause of my increased willingness to make a scene while traveling in Europe. Some of them believe it may have something to do with the rising influence of hard-liners in the Senate or perhaps with the emergence of Eurocommunism. (The latter analysis is based on the theory that patriotic Americans who used to avoid scenes in Western Europe because the Europeans might have got mad enough to become Communists no longer feel the need to be well-behaved, since the Europeans are Communists anyway.) There are analysts who believe that the decline of the dollar and the rise of the Arabs may have liberated some American tourists who felt sensitive about being embarrassingly rich. European hotel managers and headwaiters and airline managers do not know why I am increasingly willing to make a scene. All they know is that I'm a terror.

I hope the reason for my increased belligerence is in some way geopolitical. The alternative would be that I'm simply getting old and crotchety. With age, of course, comes a certain amount of sophistication. I would like to think that on those moments when I rise from the table in order to maintain a dignified stance while dressing down the headwaiter for wretched wine and stringy veal, I am less likely than I once was to spoil the effect by permitting my tie to fall into the *soup du jour* on the way up. I would like to think that I am also less likely than I once was at such moments to be addressing the busboy by mistake.

For whatever reason, I am now a maker of scenes. I have become skilled enough, in fact, to be able to observe the effect of the shouting match with some detachment while it is going on—even though the person I'm observing shouting the loudest happens to be me. I now have the sort of expertise at scenemaking that the average French sommelier has in passing off his worst wines on Americans who are unwilling to make a scene. Because of the generosity of spirit for which I am known—a generosity of spirit that might not have been evident to the last hotel manager I shouted at about the cramped and grimy room for which he presumed to charge a sum that could adequately support a Spanish family of four in moderate circumstances for a year—I intend to share that expertise with my fellow citizens. I have in mind principally my fellow male citizens: the two areas that seem invulnerable so far to the movement for women's liberation are emptying the garbage and sending back the wine. I have gathered the following tips mainly for the American husband who, through timidity or ineptness, has been unable to become a truly effective troublemaker—the man who has found his $3,000 trips to Europe marred somewhat by the tendency of his wife to say at least once a day, "Charlie, why do you have to be such a klutz?"

§ It is basic that, just before the scene is going to start, you inform your wife that this might be a nice time for her to take a stroll in the garden. You don't want her around saying, "Charlie! Remember your heart!" or if you happen to have the other sort of wife, "Charlie, stop making such an absolute ass out of yourself this instant!" Also, your honesty and integrity is undoubtedly one of the pillars her life is built on, and it might upset her to hear you make some statements that she knows are not precisely true—the statement about your connection with the house of Rothschild, for instance. You may think that your wife has some skill herself in embellishing facts while keeping a straight face, but my research on the subject indicates that there is not a woman in America who can refrain from looking a bit surprised when her husband refers to her constantly in conversation with a hotel manager as *"la principessa."*

§ The only proper language to make a scene in is English. I don't mean that a bit of the vernacular can't be effective for minor skirmishes. In Spain many years ago, an American traveler I'll call Andrew D. Kopkind—whose Spanish consisted almost entirely of a Francisco Franco quotation he had memorized, for antic reasons, from a billboard at the French border—cut down a woman who was trying to sneak into a bullfight-ticket line by saying to her, in the same frosty Spanish the *Caudillo* might have used to quote himself, "Madam, there is no liberty except within order." For the large battles, though, it is obviously wise to follow the example of General de Gaulle, who insisted on negotiating in French for reasons that are clear to anyone who ever observed the majesty of Pope Paul VI evaporate as he attempted to address some of his flock on television in English. The notion, popular in the 1950s, that an American should have enough respect for people to speak to them in their own language while in their own country is fine when applied to conversations with shoeshine boys. It was never meant to apply to conversations with hotel managers, headwaiters, or the man who just sent your baggage to Naples by mistake and suggests that you inquire after it at the lost and found window of the Naples airport. If they cannot speak English, they can always find an underling to act as interpreter. It is not a bad idea to make occasional corrections in the underling's use of the subjunctive.

§ Rank and station are still important in Europe. If Europeans believed in true, American-style democracy, after all, they would have emigrated long ago to some place like the South Side of Chicago. A computer programmer from Columbus who is taking his first trip to Europe, on the occasion of his wife's 30th birthday, need not emphasize those details when he lodges a complaint with the hotel manager of some luxurious resort hotel whose laundering staff has destroyed what were once three of the hippest rugby shirts in central Ohio. As the manager stops by the computer programmer's table on his nightly courtesy-rounds of the dining room, the computer programmer should rise from the table and begin, "Although the *principessa* and I have, of course, stayed in many hotels of this category, never before. . . ." He should then hope that the manager's reply will not be, "Excuse me, sir, but you appear to have your necktie in the soup."

The Good Old Days

August 25, 1979

Once I arrived in Canada, where we live in the summer, my view of the gasoline shortage in the United States reduced itself to one sentence: Tough luck, guys. In Canada, we (a pronoun I use casually when it suits my purposes) have no gasoline shortage—because the province of Alberta has so much oil that its Prime Minister is known as "the blue-eyed Arab." I was surprised at how quickly I abandoned any concern for my fellow Americans, including friends and blood relatives, who were left behind to suffer on the home front. As I remember, it only took about ten minutes—although, since I was still cranky from sitting in gas lines on the other side of the border, I was probably not in the best condition to note details precisely. I don't know why these indications of weak character continue to surprise me; they pop up regularly. There was a time, for instance, when I strongly believed and often stated that nepotism was despicable and that any parent who used influence to seek favoritism for his child was bringing shame on both of them. Some twenty minutes after our first child was born, I realized that I had discarded those beliefs without so much as an "on the other hand." My wife was a bit disappointed that I would abandon my principles in only twenty minutes; apparently, some new fathers with real character have held out for as long as an hour and a half.

I know there are those who will attribute my callousness toward my countrymen's suffering to sour grapes. It is true that not long before I fled the country I did a bit of investigative theorizing that I had reason to believe would be followed up by those in authority. By May, I had come to realize that the problem we faced was not merely waiting in gasoline lines but having to hear stories about waiting in gasoline lines. I realized that the entire society was being transformed into the very people we have all tried most assiduously to avoid all of our lives—the man who enjoys talking about how many miles he gets to the gallon and the man who describes in detail the route that allowed him to make it from the door of his house on East 94th to Montauk in two hours and fourteen minutes, which happens to be precisely the amount of time his description of the route requires. Publicly, I revealed the conclusion of my investigation: The Arabs, putting a Byzantine twist on the old Communist device of boring opponents into a stupor, had conspired to put us into a position to bore *ourselves* into a stupor.

I kept digging. My next breakthrough came partly from hearing someone on a Canadian radio program say that, given the decline of the dollar in international purchasing power, the increase in the price of OPEC crude oil over the past decade has been no greater than the general rate of inflation. I was reminded of a talk I had recently with a friend I often used to have lunch with when both of us had just arrived in New York. We almost always ate in a basement French restaurant in the West 40s, and we recalled that the lunch menu offered appetizer, entree, bread and butter, dessert and coffee for $1.15. Remembering the prices at the restaurant naturally led to some discussion of our equally modest salaries and how we managed "in those days"—when suddenly I blurted out, "Wait a minute! We're not talking about the turn of the century. That was 1957. There were motorcars on the streets. There were transcontinental airplanes. Frank Sinatra was a star. The *Today* program was on Channel 4." For the first time, I realized the real cause of the nostalgia explosion: Since money is the base line for any discussion of American society, inflation has accelerated the aging process of The Good Old Days.

Obviously, an important element of the acceleration has been the price of gasoline. Shortly before I escaped from my native land this spring, I heard an acquaintance reminiscing in some detail about the days when we just drove around the corner and filled up our cars with high-test for 34 cents a gallon. (My acquaintance is a simple fellow, and probably had no way of knowing that by bending my ear in that way he was serving the geopolitical aims of the United Arab Emirates.) I now realize that the old days he was talking about were in 1971. A different sort of conspiracy may be afoot, and I can only hope that the authorities investigate it with more diligence than they showed in pursuing the Great Arabian Stupor Plot. Since nostalgia is fueled by inflation, could it be that inflation is the result of a conspiracy by the people who are trying to palm off McGovern buttons and Howdy Doody puppets and their Aunt Thelma's toaster as antiques? Has there been any contact at all between OPEC and the flea-market industry?

I can now envision a time when inflation is spinning time around so quickly that fourth graders become sloppily nostalgic while talking about The Good Old Days when Hershey bars only cost 50 cents—a reference to the previous September. That would be a particularly nasty blow to Canadians, since many of the manufactured goods bought in Canada come from the United States. It's no fun being nostalgic about someone else's Hershey bar. There is already inflation in Canada, of course, but, I am relieved to report, the purchasing power of Americans living in Canada in the summer has still not been seriously affected, since the Canadian dollar is currently worth about 15 cents less than ours—a pronoun I use casually when it suits my purposes.

On the Road

September 29, 1979

There I am, bombing down Interstate 95, thinking my usual six-lane interstate kind of thoughts. I am wondering how much larger the pyramids might be if there had been a pyramid construction industry lobby for the Pharaohs to contend with. I am considering whether those in charge of the next gas-crisis allocation plan might be made to see the wisdom of a system that allowed people with even-numbered license plates to buy gas on even-numbered days, people with odd-numbered license plates to buy gas on odd-numbered days, and people with their names or initials spelled out on their license plates to buy no gas at all.

The children are in the back seat, continuing their odd custom of not arguing about who is encroaching on whose side of the seat. I know that in the view of some of my Eastern analytical friends I should worry about this. It is true that as children, my sister and I covered thousands of miles of the Great American West ignoring mountains and mesas and buttes (if they are different from mesas) and Indian-moccasin stands and roadside zoos and Burma-Shave signs and whatever else was visible out the window in order to give our complete concentration to guarding our territory. I imagine one of my Eastern analytical friends asking me if I'm worried about the possibility that our girls might be sublimating natural sibling hostilities that should be expressed. I imagine another of my Eastern analytical friends asking me if we feel guilty about not imbuing our children with the sort of contentiousness that will allow them to persevere in a world dominated by delicatessen lines. I think of myself telling both of my Eastern analytical friends to buzz off, and I keep bombing down Interstate 95.

Alice is sitting beside me in the front seat, watching me glance nervously at the state-police car in the rear-view mirror, and asking me again why I am so afraid of policemen. Alice, being a romantic, used to think that my feeling that all policemen were after me came from my experience as a reporter in the South, but I finally admitted that it comes from my experience as a teen-ager in Kansas City. Talk about traits imbued during childhood! Every teenage American boy knows that the police are lying in wait to catch him going three miles over the speed limit (posted on a smudged sign behind a thick hedge)—allowing the viciously anti-teen-age judges to strip him of his God-given right to drive. Every teen-age American girl who doesn't look like a teen-age American boy knows that the policeman who stops her for an illegal left turn that snarled traffic for six blocks is likely to put on the stern look that he has been told makes him resemble a slightly heavier Gary Cooper and say something like, "Well, you promise me you'll be real careful in the future, little lady, because we sure wouldn't want anything to happen to you."

It occurs to me, bombing down Interstate 95, that pressure on police forces to hire women and gays will eventually change all of this. A female motorcycle cop will stop a teen-age girl for a bad turn and say, "Don't give me that helpless-little-me smile, sister; I wrote the book on that one." A gay state trooper will stop a teen-age boy for going 80 in a 50-mile-per-hour zone and let him go with a warning—asking the teen-ager, while returning his driver's license, if anybody had ever told him he looks a lot like James Dean. For the time being, I am still glancing nervously at the state-trooper car in the rear-view mirror.

I pass a Cadillac Seville and feel a twinge of envy—not for the Seville but for the trip computer that I know, from an article in the *Times,* may be ticking away inside of it. When Cadillac announced that the Seville's options would henceforth include a computer, I naturally belittled the entire project. A computer, we are always being told, is only as good as what is programmed into it, and I figured the Cadillac folks could be counted on to apply the same corporate wisdom to computer programming that they once applied to the need for fender fins. Sure enough, the *Times* said that one bit of information that could be conjured up from the computer at the press of a button was how many miles the Seville was getting to the gallon—a figure that these days is likely to traumatize a Cadillac driver to the point of making him a danger to navigation. The *Times* said the computer could also calculate "speed in revolutions per minute" and "engine temperature in degrees"—just the sorts of things I have no interest in whatsoever. I was once told of a squeamish man who liked to envision his insides as being very much like the inside of a potato, and I prefer to envision the inside of automobiles exactly the same way. The Cadillac folks, I said at the time, never seem to have me in mind when they make one of their little improvements. Their market research people have never captured my profile, or, more likely, their market research people know my likes and dislikes precisely and also know that I am fated never to trade up from a Volkswagen Rabbit.

I have to admit, though, as I bomb down Interstate 95, that I covet the Seville's computer. There is no reason, after all, why the computer's program could not be varied. Instead of calculating the estimated time of arrival, "based on the variables of speed, stops, etc.," it could calculate when I will next have to stop to let my younger daughter go to the bathroom, based on the variables of 7-Up intake, nagging, and parental insensitivity. It could be of great comfort to me if it were programmed to tell me the next time we could, according to the percentages, expect to have our luggage rack fall off the car—surely a date blessedly far in the future for a family that has, the computer knows, already had its luggage rack fall off the car once. Having fed the computer statistics gathered from the Law Enforcement Assistance Administration and the American Civil Liberties Union, I could punch a few buttons and see what my chances were of encountering a gay state trooper. Thinking of the possibilities of a properly programmed computer, I am bombing down Interstate 95.

Growing Up to Be President

October 20, 1979

Every American child—at least every male, white, Christian American child—is told that, this being the land of opportunity, he could grow up to be the President of the United States. What they don't tell him is that he doesn't have to be the President of the United States if he doesn't want to be. There are other respectable callings. It is obvious, in fact, that a young man who showed promise at being able to slice up an enzyme or put together an inspired clam chowder would be wasting his talents as President. The second-grade teacher never talks about that part of it, though, so every little white Christian boy in the class thinks he is the one who is supposed to be the President. That is why little white Christian boys often seem so much less interesting than little black or Jewish or Chicano or Chinese boys, or than any sort of little girls: little white Christian boys are under a lot of White House pressure. Almost none of them, of course, do grow up to be the President of the United States, and those who don't naturally feel disappointed. When a man who was led to believe that he might have "Hail to the Chief" played every time he entered a room realizes that he is going to spend his life in outer offices hoping to get a few minutes of the assistant buyer's time, there is bound to be a certain letdown.

It may be that the malaise recently discovered in our national soul by White House poll taker Patrick Caddell, the Melancholy Drone, is not what it appeared to be at the time—the malaise that might be found among the passengers of an ocean liner whose captain seems to be steering it in smaller and smaller circles—but simply the effect of there being so many white Christian males who are depressed by their belief that they ought to be President and aren't, compounded by their belief that Jimmy Carter oughtn't to be President and is.

The presence of Carter in the White House, of course, is based on the belief that the proprietor of any middle-sized agribusiness can rise to the Presidency if he simply works hard, studies at night with his wife to broaden their cultural horizons, and keeps a low profile during civil rights disputes. Carter was apparently given a sort of booster shot in this type of thinking while he was Governor of Georgia. According to the authorized version of how he happened to have the confidence to undertake what seemed like a hopeless race for the White House, Carter was visited by most of the national political figures who passed through Georgia during his governorship, and he decided, after observing them carefully, that if they could be national political figures, he could be a national political figure too. Alas, he underestimated them. In taking the measure of his nationally known houseguests over dinner at the Governor's mansion, he failed to consider one factor: if a national political figure has spent the entire day with the

Young Democrats of Georgia, and has then been denied a drink before dinner because the Devil's brew is not permitted within the mansion's walls, and has then been subjected to a two-hour dinner-table lecture on the beatific qualities of state-government reorganization, that national political figure is not likely to be quite himself.

While reading all of this depressing talk of national depression—not to speak of a National Depression—it has occurred to me that one advantage of a monarchy is that a monarchy does not suffer the effects of having great clots of white Christians moping around simply because they aren't the king or the queen. (The other advantage of a monarchy is that the monarch never auctions off his memoirs, with an escalating clause on subsidiary rights.) In Britain, for instance, everyone knows that you can't grow up to be the King or the Queen unless you happen to grow up in Buckingham Palace. Nobody wants to grow up to be the Prime Minister. The Prime Minister doesn't even have a helicopter.

As a child growing up in Kansas City, I was subjected to an undiluted dose of the anyone-can-be-President tonic. For part of my childhood, after all, Harry Truman, someone everybody in town claimed to have known as a failed haberdasher on Thirty-First and Main, was, in fact, the President. Also, my father, who had been brought to Missouri from Eastern Europe as an infant, had the new American's confidence that absolutely anyone, regardless of race or creed or color, could grow up to be President—particularly me. I now realize why he was so casual about assuming that I should have Presidential expectations: Being ineligible because of his foreign birth, he didn't have to worry about becoming President himself.

When I was about 14, I decided against seeking the Presidency. Fourteen being an impressionable age, I was accustomed to making such major decisions on the basis of a picture in a magazine or a line in a film. Around the same time, I had decided against a career in the law when I saw someone in a movie—someone like Clark Gable—snap shut his briefcase, jam on his hat, and say, as he walked out of the room, "I'll have my lawyers draw up the papers." I had no intention of being the person who, instead of saying that, said, "Christ! Now I'll have to go back to the office and draw up the wretched papers."

My Presidential ambitions were ended by a phrase in the Kansas City *Star:* "The President is expected to submit his budget next week." Until then, I hadn't thought of the President doing anything like a budget. Waving to cheering crowds and shaking hands with the March of Dimes poster child were more the sort of things I had in mind. I hate budgets. I informed my father that I was no longer available. My father was, of course, disappointed, but, having observed me for a while with the same care Jimmy Carter later employed to observe visiting national political figures, he seemed to have adopted as a fall-back aspiration for me the hope that I would somehow escape becoming a ward of the county. I am still not certain how to avoid these problems with my own children. For the moment, I am telling them that in this country anyone can grow up to impeach the President.

Invading Cuba

November 10, 1979

"Daddy, why did the Marines invade Cuba?"

"Invade Cuba! Marines! Why doesn't anyone ever tell me anything?"

"Didn't you promise Mommy you'd quit answering questions with questions?"

"Did I?"

"Yes."

"For breakfast this morning, we are offering Cheerios, Product 19, some yucky health cereal and Rice Krispies. The management wishes to inform you that the Rice Krispies, while completely inert if left to themselves, will react to the addition of milk by going snap, crackle and, occasionally, pop—and so may not be advisable for those who have particularly severe hangovers."

"Little girls don't get hangovers, Daddy."

"Ah, the miraculous recuperative powers of the young."

"Daddy, please answer my question: Why did the Marines invade Cuba? It says right here 'Marines charge ashore at Guantánamo Bay.' "

"Well, you see, Guantánamo Bay is a part of Cuba that really isn't Cuba. A long time ago, that part was turned over to us for a Navy base so we could protect Cuba from its enemies."

"Who are Cuba's enemies?"

"We are."

"Is that why the Marines invaded Guantánamo Bay?"

"Oh no. The Marines invaded Guantánamo Bay because there are Russian troops in the part of Cuba that really is Cuba, and we don't want them there."

"Then why didn't the Marines invade the Cuba part of Cuba?"

"Because there are Russian troops there. Someone could be hurt. Are you sure you wouldn't rather discuss whether or not a bowl of Cheerios fulfills your minimum daily requirement of preservatives?"

"Why are the Russian troops in Cuba anyway?"

"Well, the Russians have an arrangement with Fidel Castro. He sends soldiers to fight anyone they want fought in Africa, because the Russian troops all come from a northern climate, and if they went to Africa themselves they would be particularly susceptible to heat rash. In return, the Russians give him eight million dollars a day plus some soldiers to sit around and drink rum. You see, the Cubans are used to having foreigners sit around drinking rum; there have always been foreigners sitting around Cuba drinking rum. Castro is afraid that if there aren't any the people will get restless or will think they're in Finland or someplace and become dangerously confused."

"Who is Fidel Castro?"

"He is the leader of the Nonaligned Nations."

"But I thought you said that he did what the Russians tell him to do. How can he be nonaligned?"

"Your mother's a wizard at foreign affairs. Are you sure

this isn't the sort of thing you ought to talk to her about, woman to woman?"

"That was a question in reply to a question."

"O.K. You asked for it. You see, there are a lot of people in America who look for Communists under their beds. Political scientists call them Dust Ballers, because what they usually find under their beds is not Communists but those little balls of dust that always get under beds. When all they find year after year is dust balls, the Dust Ballers get very depressed. Fidel Castro is a very kind man who tries to arrange things so that the Dust Ballers are right now and then. When he first took over in Cuba, the Dust Ballers said he was a Communist, but everyone else said they were being silly and even Castro said they were being silly. Then, after a while, he said that he had his fingers crossed when he said he wasn't a Communist: He was a Communist after all. The Dust Ballers were very happy for a while, but then for the next fifteen years or so they found mainly dust balls. They would say that Nonaligned Nations were nothing but Communists, and everyone would make fun of them. Castro heard about it, so he became the official leader of the Nonaligned Nations so that the Dust Ballers could be right again. When it comes to the Dust Ballers, Castro's a real softy."

"But what does having the Russian troops in Cuba have to do with the Marines invading their own base?"

"Well, we wanted to show them that we're tough. If they have a combat brigade in there, we'll invade our own base. If they put a fleet there, we'll attack one of our ports. If they put in offensive missiles there again, we'll destroy

Schenectady, New York, with intercontinental ballistic missiles. It's called 'measured response.' "

"Could I have some milk on my Rice Krispies?"

"It does make an awful racket."

"I don't have a hangover, Daddy."

"You're not the only one here."

"Daddy, is invading your own base kind of like the man you told me about in the Rose Bowl who got the ball and ran over his own goal line?"

"Oh no. He thought he was going the right way. The Marines knew they were invading their own base. You see, when the Secretary of State learned that there were Russian troops in Cuba, he didn't know that they were just there to drink rum. So he said the status quo was unacceptable. Something had to change or we would be so mad at Russia that we would quit accepting all the Russian ballet stars and athletes who defect after they're over the hill, and the Russians would be stuck with paying all that pension money. So what changed was that we invaded our own base."

"What did the Russians do?"

"They went out on a ship and watched."

"To spy?"

"Oh no. The Russians watched because they had never seen anybody invade his own base before. They thought it would be a good break from just sitting around drinking rum. When we decide to destroy Schenectady, I suspect they'll sell tickets."

The Great Debate

December 1, 1979

Washington, Sept. 14—Any hope that the Presidential campaign debates would not be dominated by talk of Senator Kennedy's alleged philandering and Governor Reagan's alleged age was dashed in Tuesday night's initial encounter when Senator Kennedy said, in response to a probing question about skirt-chasing, "I don't do that sort of thing anymore," and Governor Reagan broke in to say, "I do! I do!"

Those who value the campaign debates as an institution were disheartened not only by the level of the discussion but by the behavior of Rafferty O'Leary, the Boston political reporter, who stirred suspicion of a Kennedy bias from his first question to Governor Reagan ("Governor, don't you think, when it gets right down to it, you're just too old to cut the mustard?"). A suspicion of bias became a suspicion of collusion when O'Leary, later in the debate, asked the Governor, "Governor Reagan, is it true that you dye your nose?"

Most observers here believe that Mr. O'Leary, who was making his first appearance on national television, meant to ask Governor Reagan about his hair rather than his nose, and simply misread the question, having left his eyeglasses at home in the belief that they would detract from his appearance. There are also people in Washington who believe that a genuine confusion arose in Mr. O'Leary's mind because in his home town of Boston some politicians, intent on disguising the broken blood vessels and telltale scarlet that sometimes accompany heavy drinking, actually *do* dye their noses. Certainly, there is no significant body of opinion here in support of the contention that Governor Reagan dyes his nose. To this reporter, who was in the studio during the debate, the Governor's nose seemed consistent in color with the rest of his face.

Whatever the facts on the Governor's nose color—and, in this campaign in which no issue seems out of bounds, the nation's voters are entitled to expect a full airing of those facts—O'Leary's apparent mistake raised the ugly possibility that the question he read was not his own. Under the circumstances, it is incumbent on the Kennedy camp to reveal whether O'Leary's connection with Senator Kennedy extends beyond what is already widely known—that he has been a frequent guest at the Senator's McLean, Virginia, estate and that he works there on weekends as an assistant groom.

Both candidates were well prepared. Governor Reagan only twice had to consult a tattered copy of the speech he used to deliver for General Electric. Kennedy's staff work was most impressive in the Senator's handling of a surprise question asked by Rob Pretty of ABC about a seventeen-year-old magazine feature on his wife ("A New Mrs. Kennedy in Washington," *Look,* February 26, 1963), which included a picture of Mrs. Kennedy in the Senator's old Army field jacket. Pretty, ABC chief investigative reporter, had unearthed not only the old *Look* article but the fact that the field jacket is the one item of clothing all soldiers are required to hand in upon discharge.

"I'm glad you asked that, Rob," the Senator said. "I think the Army Regulation you're referring to is A.R. 47-328-HR3b. Roscoe Felkner, who was the supply clerk of my outfit, has now signed an affidavit swearing that he neglected to call that A.R. to my attention. We also have a statement from Arthur Schlesinger, Jr., the distinguished historian, who says that both Andrew Jackson and Theodore Roosevelt failed to hand in their field jackets, and that they were better Presidents for it. Mr. Felkner can be contacted at my McLean, Virginia, estate, where he works as an assistant groom."

Senator Kennedy's answer was so complete that Pretty, it has now been revealed, decided against asking a follow-up question about whether the sort of Army inspection tours common to the Presidency would present the Senator with irresistible temptations to let a machine gun stick to his fingers or to make off with an ICBM.

Although the Senator has insisted that his Presidential campaign staff is not made up of "old Kennedy hands," Schlesinger is not the only such hand whose presence was felt in the debate. Theodore Sorensen, who is known for what students of American political oratory refer to as "reversible raincoat sentences" ("Ask not what your country can do for you, ask . . ."), has supposedly chosen not to interrupt his career in private life to join the campaign—he works at the Senator's McLean, Virginia, estate as an assistant groom—but his touch seemed apparent when Senator Kennedy said, in answering the sixth of twenty-three questions he was asked about Chappaquiddick, "Although I feared to drown, I drowned my fear." The remark went unnoticed by most viewers, as it happened, because Governor Reagan chose that moment to interrupt again, interjecting, "I'm a helluva swimmer. Helluva swimmer. I can swim circles around that tub of guts."

Governor Reagan, who has concentrated on projecting an image of youthful vigor, may have carried that strategy too far by arriving at the National Broadcasting Company's New York studios for the debate on horseback, and refusing to dismount. Senator Kennedy was wise to take no notice of the fact that his opponent was debating on horseback ("It would have only drawn attention to him," the Senator said later, "and that was what he was after"). It was characteristic of the bitterness already engendered by this campaign that Governor Reagan's staff reacted to the Governor's fall by accusing Senator Kennedy of having startled the horse by pounding the lectern for emphasis after answering a question about his involvement in the short-sheeting of the bed of the assistant headmaster of Milton Academy in 1946. To this observer, who was in the studio, it appeared that the horse simply reared in the heat of rebuttal. It now remains to be seen who stands to gain politically from the fact that Senator Kennedy, as he walked out of the NBC studio, was detained by New York police for leaving the scene of an accident.

Another Great Debate

December 22, 1979

Washington, Sept. 19—Those of us who complained about the first of the Presidential campaign debates having been dominated by talk of Senator Kennedy's alleged philandering and Governor Reagan's alleged age were, of course, disappointed last night when, at the very beginning of the second debate, a perfectly legitimate request that Senator Kennedy outline his views on foreign affairs caused the Senator to flush and then stamp off the stage in anger, leaving Governor Reagan to shout, "Don't think I can't match him French bimbo for French bimbo!"

The only significant new issue brought up last night—an acknowledgment that Senator Kennedy's tortured syntax is causing some voters uneasiness about the level of his intelligence—was raised almost accidentally when, in answer to a pointed question about separation of powers, the Senator named two branches of Government and then paused, obviously unable to think of the third. Governor Reagan was well within his rights to use the incident later in the debate ("Is that the sort of thing he's planning to say to Brezhnev on the hot line—'It's right here on the tip of my tongue?' "), but it did seem unsportsmanlike to break the awkward silence of Senator Kennedy's long pause by shouting "Who's going to take *this* quiz for you, Teddy?" The Governor's remark was made to appear prescient rather than rude, though, when Senator Kennedy managed to recall the judiciary only after reading a note delivered from the audience by Arthur Schlesinger, Jr.

Ironically, Senator Kennedy's lapse of memory came at a time when Governor Reagan had raised some doubts about his own grasp of world events by beginning a list of foreign heads of state who are older than he is with the names of Francisco Franco, Syngman Rhee, Bernard Baruch and Connie Mack. Certainly there is no support in the scientific community for Governor Reagan's contention that if Abraham Lincoln's life had not been cut short by an assassin's bullet he would now be 160 years old. Mentioning Eubie Blake, the renowned jazz composer and performer, as a possible Secretary of the Treasury seemed a transparent attempt by Governor Reagan to link his celebration of the energy and vitality of some older Americans with an appeal to the black vote. Mr. Blake, who is twenty-four years past the mandatory retirement age for Federal employees, was wise to state immediately after the debate that he had no interest whatsoever in being Secretary of the Treasury ("nickels and dimes, nickels and dimes").

Last night's encounter raised some serious questions about the performance of both candidates and about the pattern that could develop in the remaining sixteen debates. Certainly it can be considered progress that Governor Reagan did not insist on debating on horseback last night, although that might be explained by the injury his horse suffered in the first debate. There is reason to be grateful that the questioners last night seemed less interested in Chappaquiddick, asking Senator Kennedy only nineteen questions on that subject—all of which were answered by Paul Markham and Joseph Gargan, speaking in chorus. But will Governor Reagan continue to remove his shirt when questions of age come up ("Take a look at the delts and lats of a man half my age!")? Will Rafferty O'Leary, the Boston political writer with some connections to the Kennedy family, continue his hostile line of questions to Governor Reagan ("You're trying to tell the American people, then, that those are all your own teeth?")?

Although Democratic professionals are not saying outright that they are disappointed in Senator Kennedy's performance so far, it may be significant that they spend a lot of time talking about how Jimmy Carter could have had the nomination if only his attempts to punish Mayor Jane Byrne for defecting to Senator Kennedy had stopped at closing the main post office in Chicago. It is now painfully obvious to the Carter camp that most Americans simply did not agree with White House Chief of Staff Hamilton Jordan that withdrawing the air traffic controllers from O'Hare Airport was "nothing more than plain old hardball politics."

At the same time, Republican strategists think Governor Reagan may have committed a serious tactical error in making such an issue out of Arthur Schlesinger, Jr. Governor Reagan obviously has the right to call attention to Mr. Schlesinger's remarks—made in the August 1979 issue of *McCall's*—that Chappaquiddick would make Senator Kennedy a better President because it resulted in an effort at self-redemption that "may be for Teddy Kennedy what polio was for F.D.R." It is less clear that Mr. Schlesinger actually said, as the Reagan forces claim, that "Teddy Kennedy's Chappaquiddick and George Washington's Valley Forge were essentially the same sort of experience, except for taking place at different seasons of the year." In any case, revealing a passage from Mr. Schlesinger's undergraduate Harvard diary, which the Reagan forces apparently obtained through the Freedom of Information Act, seems to have no purpose beyond embarrassing Mr. Schlesinger and titillating the public—particularly if, as Washington rumors have it, Mr. Schlesinger may soon leave the campaign to devote full time to his two-volume history of Elaine's. The passage that Governor Reagan had no justification for quoting is as follows: "Dear Diary, Today I asked those cool Kennedy boys again if I could play in their touch football game on the quad and they said again that I was a wonk and a weenie and a wimp and a grind and walked like a duck. I told them that someday I would be a famous historian and if they ever let me play with them then I would write *whatever they wanted me to write.*"

Backwards Ran the Clock

February 2, 1980

On a Wednesday afternoon just before Christmas, the wall clock in our kitchen began to run backward. I'm not talking about a literary device here; I'm talking about a clock. Suddenly, this clock's sweep second hand was moving in a direction that can only be described as counterclockwise. There were witnesses. Alice was having a meeting in the living room—part of what seems to be an effort to make our house competitive with the Sheraton Convention Center, presumably so that we may someday take a write-off on our ashtrays. The washing machine repairman was present. In fact, there are those who say that he had something to do with the clock's sudden switch in direction, since he was fiddling with the circuit breakers upstairs. But the washing machine repairman is almost always at our house, fiddling with the circuit breakers upstairs. He likes to fiddle with circuit breakers. The only piece of modern technology that repels him is the automatic washer.

The wall clock in our kitchen does not have numbers. It has letters that spell out Hecker's Flour, except for the apostrophe. Having a clock with only letters on it means that my daughters, before they learned to tell time, would occasionally say something like "the little hand's on the R and the big hand is just past the C,'' but I do not consider that a strong disadvantage in a clock. The face of our clock can be illuminated by two light bulbs with a glow so strong that I used to assume pilots were using it at night to take a bead on La Guardia. We no longer keep light bulbs in the clock, because my daughters say that would be a waste of energy. As I interpret my daughters' views on the energy crisis, they believe that a patriotic American household should use no energy except that required to power a computer game called Merlin and a Tyco Super-Dooper-Double-Looper Auto Track. In addition to knowing a lot about how much fossil fuel we're wasting, my daughters are already learned on the subject of cholesterol in Italian sausage and carcinogens in beer. Their command of a broad range of such information, in fact, has made it obvious to me why some children in our public elementary schools have difficulty reading and writing: their teachers spend most of the day teaching them how to depress their parents.

Our clock was a gift from Pat Uhlmann, a friend of ours from Kansas City. Pat is very conservative politically—perhaps the most politically conservative man ever to be mentioned with affection in a left-wing magazine—but he is a left-liberal when it comes to distributing clocks and other handouts, even to the sort of people who have made it clear by now that they have no intention of pulling themselves up by their own bootstraps. Having once seen Pat remove and offer me a necktie that Alice (though not I) had admired, I think I can honestly say that he is generous to a fault. When the clock started running backward, we may have been overheard making a few innocent remarks about the possibility that its behavior simply reflected the direction in which Pat sometimes seems to want the world to go. A few days later, we received a letter from Pat saying, "Even a stopped clock is right twice a day, which is more than I can say for you." Our clock was not stopped, of course; it was running backward.

One morning at breakfast, my younger daughter asked me if it would soon be yesterday. I told her it would be if we were talking about a literary device rather than a clock. She asked me why the clock was running backward, and I told her to pay more attention to her cereal-eating, my alternative being to admit to her that the only explanation I had been able to think of was that our clock had been invaded by a dybbuk, a bloody-minded cousin of the dybbuk in our washing machine. It happened to be a time when I was feeling the weight of my ignorance more acutely than usual. I had only just learned who Donna Summer was. I had not distinguished myself in the assembling of the Tyco Super-Dooper-Double-Looper Auto Track. I had just been forced to admit to my older daughter that I did not know how to get the square root of anything. All in all, I would have preferred a clock that ran in the conventional direction. Not knowing enough Yiddish to speak to the dybbuk in his native tongue, I tried to reason quietly with him in what I perceived to be English of Yiddish inflection ("So go! I'll pack you a lunch"), but the clock continued to run backward.

In this mood, I went to my next-door neighbor's for a cup of seasonal cheer, and met a friend who said she was worried about the world because Afghanistan had the H-bomb. This was several weeks before the Russian adventure, and Afghanistan was not a country often mentioned when holiday discussions ventured from the Brandy Alexander recipe toward sophisticated weapons systems.

"Afghanistan does not have the H-bomb," I assured her.

"They've got it," she said. "I read it in the *Times.*"

"There's a progression in these matters," I said. "First a country gets a drugstore. Then it gets the H-bomb."

"I saw it in the *Times,*" she repeated. "The leader of Afghanistan has slicked-down hair and one of those waxed mustaches. I know he wouldn't use it right."

"General Zia!" I said. "That's Pakistan."

She was comforted, and I felt more in control for a while—until I began to wonder what was so comforting about Pakistan's having the H-bomb. Would they use it right? What was the right way to use it?

It was in this mood that I happened to mention our clock to Noam Spanier, who goes to Stuyvesant High School—a seat of learning so high-powered that it offers courses other than Serum Cholesterol 121 and Ravages of Booze 202.

"Your polarity is reversed," Noam said.

"Watch your mouth, kid," I said, taking a quick check of my clothing.

We went next door. Noam unplugged my clock, turned the plug around, and plugged it in again. The clock began to run clockwise.

"Obviously," I said.

Noam nodded.

"It's obvious," I repeated. "You scared the hell out of the dybbuk."

The Case of the Purloined Turkey

March 15, 1980

A secretly Xeroxed manuscript of Richard Nixon's new book has, as they say in the trade, found its way into my possession. For years, I have been waiting for some carefully guarded document to find its way into my possession. In my mind, the phrase has always conjured up the vision of an important document wandering the streets of lower Manhattan, confused and bewildered, until a kindly policeman on Sixth Avenue provides flawless directions to my house. I figured that a secret document would find its way into my possession if I simply waited around long enough at the same address, looking receptive. That is precisely what happened. I did not ferret out this document. I might as well admit that I hadn't realized Mr. Nixon had produced another volume; it seemed only moments since the last one. I had assumed, I suppose, that his literary output would have been slowed up by the bustle of moving from San Clemente and by his previous difficulties with trying to buy an apartment in East Side co-ops that persisted in treating him as if he were Jewish or a tap-dancer. Ordinarily, complications involving living quarters play havoc with a writer's production; a writer I'll call William Edgett Smith, whose procrastination devices are taught in the senior creative writing seminar at Princeton, once stopped writing for seven weeks in order to see to a leaky radiator. Mr. Nixon apparently suffered no such delays—although in Smith's defense it should be said that he has to manage with no Federally funded research or secretarial help to speak of. Despite the interruptions that accompany any move ("The men want to know whether those partly erased tapes in the cellar stay or go, Dick, and what do you want done with the crown jewels of Rumania?"), Mr. Nixon managed to turn out a volume for Warner Books called *The Real War*. I know because a Xerox of the manuscript found its way into my possession.

Although it is customary to refuse to divulge the source of any document that has found its way into one's possession, I should say at the start that the person who gave me this document was Victor S. Navasky, the editor of *The Nation*. If anybody feels the need to prosecute or sue, Navasky's your man. I feel no compunction about shifting the blame to Navasky, because he would obviously be the logical target of any investigation anyway, this being his second caper. At this very moment *The Nation* is being sued by Harper & Row and *Reader's Digest* for $12,500 for running an article based on a smuggled-out manuscript of Gerald Ford's book, which was somehow published under a title other than *The White House Memories of a Lucky Klutz*. In an era when an unfairly dismissed busboy would never think of suing for less than a million, the purpose of suing *The Nation* for the price of a publisher's lunch is obvious: the plaintiffs want to make Navasky out to be not just a thief but a small-time thief.

My involvement in this started innocently when Navasky said to me, "We've got a copy of Nixon's book."

"I hope you didn't pay full price," I said.

"Not that book. The new one. Smuggled out."

Sticky Fingers Navasky had struck again. I was, of course, astonished. It's no joke to discover that you've been handing copy in to a recidivist. "If you put it back now, maybe they won't notice that it was missing," I said. Warner Books is part of the sort of conglomerate that is often described as "playing hardball," and I figured that they weren't above humiliating Navasky by suing him for something like $18 and carfare.

"Take it!" Navasky said, thrusting a bulky bundle into my arms. "Reveal something."

I took it, and skulked out the door. The elevator man was reading the sports page of the *Daily News* as we descended. "Just some laundry," I said to him, gesturing at the bundle I was carrying. "Shirts. That sort of thing." He kept reading. So far, so good.

When I got home, I went into my office, closed the door, and began the manuscript. The first sentence said, "As I write this, a third of a century has passed since I first entered Congress; five years have passed since I resigned the Presidency." Definitely authentic. I plunged ahead. After what seemed like about an hour, I was startled by the jangle of the telephone. It was Navasky.

"Find anything yet?" he said.

I looked down at the manuscript. I was on page 4. "He says, 'The next two decades represent a time of maximum crisis for America and for the West, during which the fate of the world for generations to come may well be determined.' "

There was silence on the phone. Then Navasky said, "Skip ahead."

I skipped ahead to page 105, and started reading. "He says, 'The final chapters have yet to be written on the war in Vietnam,' " I reported.

"Skip some more," Navasky said.

"Well," I said, "on page 287 he says, 'The President has great power in wartime as Commander in Chief of the armed forces. But he also has enormous power to prevent war and preserve peace.' "

There was a pause. "Keep skipping," Navasky said.

I read him Nixon's views on leaks ("We must find an accommodation between freedom of the press and the requirements of national survival"). Silence. I read paragraphs on the advantages of summit conferences and on the difference between totalitarianism and authoritarianism. More silence. Finally, I said, "Shall I keep skipping?"

There was no answer. Navasky had fallen asleep.

What is the purpose of being willing to reveal the contents of a purloined manuscript if there is nothing in it that bears revealing?

"Let's give it back," I said to Navasky.

"Our source does not want it back," Navasky said.

"I can see his point."

"Maybe we should shred it," Navasky said.

"All I have in that line is a Cuisinart," I said. "I have a better idea. I'll put it on Sixth Avenue. Maybe it will find its way into someone else's possession."

Sticky Fingers at Large

April 5, 1980

Sticky Fingers Navasky remains at large. Three weeks ago, in this space, I confessed that Victor S. Navasky, the editor of *The Nation,* had stolen a Xeroxed copy of the manuscript of Richard M. Nixon's new book, *The Real War* (a title drawn, of course, from the famous passage by Thucydides: "The real war is not on the field of battle, where armies clash; the real war is when they start questioning write-offs for business entertainment"). Navasky then gave the manuscript to me—I barely knew it was stolen—and instructed me to find something to reveal. It was Navasky's second offense. *The Nation* had just been sued, for an embarrassingly modest sum, by Harper & Row and *Reader's Digest*—the plaintiffs' claim being that Sticky Fingers, in reckless disregard of copyright laws and literary standards, had published material based on a hot manuscript of Gerald Ford's memoirs, which not only failed to be called *The White House Memories of a Lucky Klutz* but failed to be subtitled *Is This the Fairway for the 8th Hole or What?* Naturally, I have no desire to see Navasky put away for eight-to-twenty simply because he is a two-time loser who seems to defy every effort at rehabilitation. I had assumed, though, that the authorities would at least pick him up and work him over a bit at the station house. So far, nobody has laid a glove on him. He walks among us, indistinguishable from respectable citizens. I can only conclude that what we're facing here is a breakdown of law and order.

If the men in blue ever did put the collar on Navasky, I suppose parsimony would be his first line of defense: considering what he is accustomed to paying writers, he could claim, stealing practically any manuscript would constitute no more than petty theft. At Navasky's rates, according to my calculations, Nixon's book is worth about $137.50. The fact that Navasky stole rather than bought Nixon's prose does mean, of course, that history has been robbed of a negotiating session between Navasky and Nixon's literary agent, Irving (Swifty) Lazar. Ever since Navasky told me he was thinking about paying me "in the high two figures" for each of my efforts, I have looked forward to a head-to-head confrontation someday between him and Irving (Swifty) Lazar. As I have always seen the meeting in my mind, Irving (Swifty) Lazar bustles into Navasky's office, emitting steamy little puffs of talk about "big bucks" and "points on the gross" and "up-front money." I prefer to think that Irving (Swifty) Lazar talks that way; if he actually sounds like an associate professor of comparative literature, I don't want to know about it.

"So what we're talking here is two hundred thou on the floor bid," I imagine Irving (Swifty) Lazar saying.

Navasky looks at the floor. It needs sweeping. He clears his throat. "Well, Irving (Swifty) Lazar," he says, being one of those rare editors who knows how to pronounce a parenthesis, "we were thinking along the lines of something in the exceedingly low three figures." In a strategy meeting before the negotiating session, Navasky has decided that he is prepared to go to $140 if no unusual postage charges or long-distance telephone calls are involved. Those who accuse *The Nation* of being insufficiently patriotic could not be aware of how devoutly Navasky attempts to follow the President's guidelines on wage and price controls.

About a week ago, it occurred to me that Navasky had available to him a stronger defense than his worldwide reputation for stinginess. The realization came while I was thinking back on my experience of reading the stolen Nixon manuscript—an experience that for excitement and interest I can compare to waiting in the baggage-claim area for the suitcases to be brought from the plane. I don't mean to complain; I declined the $2.35 Navasky offered me for the extra time involved. I mention the experience only because it would enable me to testify, if properly subpoenaed and guaranteed immunity, that searching for something to reveal from *The Real War* was like searching for something to reveal from the authorized biography of the founder of the United Way Campaign of Rockford, Illinois.

I telephoned Navasky. "Don't worry," I said. "Looked at from the proper angle, stealing what you stole was quite a bit less than petty theft."

"I don't know what you mean," Navasky said.

"Let's say, for instance, that you were the mastermind of a spy ring," I said.

"I'm a loyal American," Navasky said. "A tireless fighter against the grinding inflation that saps our nation of its strength."

"But let's say that you were the mastermind of a spy ring," I said. "You've managed to recruit some code clerks and a typist or two—paying them modestly, of course, on the theory that they're getting regular salaries from the Defense Department or the C.I.A. anyway. One of them turns you in because you have enraged him by refusing to pick up the tab for the Metro rides he has to take to the drop. The F.B.I. bursts into your apartment and finds everything you have stolen: working plans for the crossbow, an 1894 report on how to put a keen edge on a cavalry saber, two First World War helmets, the formula for C-rations. This is the same thing: the manuscript you nicked is without value except for some collateral use as a sleeping aid."

There was a long silence on Navasky's end of the telephone.

"I wouldn't push your luck, though," I went on. "Don't go making off with galleys of some sensitive first novel of boyhood in Alabama or an early draft of the Interior Department's annual report on the state of the prairie dog population in Montana. Enough's enough. Also, I'd get rid of the Nixon manuscript if I were you."

"What Nixon manuscript?" Navasky said.

No wonder Sticky Fingers Navasky remains at large.

Understanding Parity

April 26, 1980

I was not alarmed when the report came from Kansas, where Governor Ronald Reagan was campaigning among wheat farmers, that he did not seem to know exactly what parity means. I don't know exactly what parity means either. I have always suspected that practically nobody knows what parity means—the possible exceptions being a few farmers and the Washington correspondent of *The Des Moines Register & Tribune*.

"I think it's shocking that a man running for President of the United States does not even know what parity means," Alice said, when she read the news from Kansas.

"I don't know what it means either," I said.

"You don't?" she said. "But didn't I hear you say yesterday that Reagan was out in the farm belt talking about cowpods and parity?"

"You did indeed," I said. "But I don't know what it means. I don't think anybody knows what it means."

I avoided the question of whether she happened to know the meaning of parity herself. I had learned my lesson some months before when, in an idle moment, I asked her the name of the Secretary of Labor and she replied, "I will not stand here and be grilled like a common criminal."

"But I've heard you argue against parity," Alice said.

"True," I admitted. "Also for it. But I don't know what it means. You don't have to know what something means to argue about it. Do you think all of those people who were arguing about populism a few years ago knew what it meant? When I was working on the college newspaper, as I remember it, I managed to write at least half a dozen editorials on something called the Oak Street Connector without having the remotest idea of what it was. I demanded to know why construction of the Oak Street Connector was behind schedule. I questioned whether the Oak Street Connector was really what the city ought to have been spending its money on. I argued against it. Also for it."

"What did it turn out to be?"

"I don't know," I said. "It still wasn't finished when I graduated; my last editorial on it complained of 'unconscionable delays.' It might be a building, I suppose, or maybe a viaduct—unless, of course, it's an electrical generator. Or a dating service."

I know Alice was distressed that I had never made an effort to find out what parity means, although she bravely tried to hide her disappointment by calling me an ignoramus. In my defense, I can only say that once, many years ago, I suffered what the social scientists would call a strong disincentive to learning the meaning of parity; I knew someone who knew precisely what parity meant, and he couldn't seem to keep it to himself. Among the staff of a magazine we were both working for a time, he was the writer who specialized in subjects like long-term financing problems of the utility industry and the legislation governing public housing—not to speak of parity. Not to speak of parity was something he rarely did in my presence. He must have known that, when it came to parity, my tabula was particularly rasa, because he seemed to respond to my presence the way a particularly zealous missionary responds to the presence of the village's most intractable idol worshipper. Listening to his explanatory drone was one of those experiences that instructs a young man in the blessings of selective ignorance.

"I think any well-informed citizen would know what parity means," Alice said, making it clear from the remark what sort of citizen she considered me.

I picked up the telephone and called a writer we know—a specialist in foreign affairs and some of the other black arts. "Ronald Reagan doesn't know what parity means," I said.

"I'm not surprised to hear it," the foreign affairs specialist said. "I have always assumed that even mild irony would be beyond his range."

"Not parody," I said. "Parity."

"Oh. Well."

"Do you?"

"Do I what?"

"Do you know what parity means?"

There was a long pause. "Agriculture is, in fact, a peripheral issue," the foreign affairs specialist said. "The only issue that touched our survival—the survival of our society, the very survival of life on this planet—is the issue of war and peace."

Just as I thought. For further confirmation, I telephoned a friend who is known to be wise in the ways of New York politics.

"Do you know what parity is?" I asked.

"Of course I know what parity is," he said. "Parity is what the farmers are always kvetching about."

"That is precisely how much any well-informed citizen knows about parity," I said to Alice. "That it has something to do with farmers. It's just like Two-Words Tofsky's old trick."

"I suppose you're going to tell me who Two-Words Tofsky is even if I don't ask," she said.

"Glad you brought it up," I said. "Two-Words Tofsky was a college acquaintance of mine who understood that anyone could sound knowledgeable about any subject if he simply knew the right two words to put together. If someone mentioned Husserl, Two-Words would say something like, 'I decided phenomenology's not for me.' Someone asked him what he thought about Thoreau once, and he said 'Too outdoorsy.' Everybody thought Two-Words knew everything."

"And where is Two-Words today?"

"Last time I saw him, he was farming wheat in Kansas."

"And does he understand what parity is?"

"Of course not," I said. "But he was doing a lot of kvetching about it. I told him the farmers would be better off to forget about parity and start concentrating on productivity."

"What did you mean by that?"

"I haven't the foggiest," I said. "I don't know what productivity means either."

Literary Swifties

May 10, 1980

For this reviewer, the tone of last night's historic television first—the first time the National Literary Awards were presented as a prime-time network program, in the manner of the film industry's Oscar ceremonies—was set by one of the early winners, Martin McCaffery, who won his "Swifty" for Best Non-Jewish First Novel with No Sex Below the Waist. Standing at the podium, his Levis and fisherman's sweater in stark contrast to the tuxedo of the presenter, Joe Namath, McCaffery grabbed the Swifty statuette firmly, leaned into the microphone, and said, "It is certainly no thanks to my rotten, chintzy, incompetent publisher that I am here tonight." Unlike the Oscar ceremonies, which have become notorious for speeches thanking long lists of associates and family and friends, the Swifty awards were remarkable in that not one winner thanked anybody for anything—although one presenter, apparently under the impression that the microphone was not on, was overheard to say, "Thank God at least they didn't get Capote to emcee."

The negotiations breakthrough that made last night's ceremonies possible, of course, came last month when those writers who had insisted that the selection of winners be done by people they were accustomed to being judged by agreed to an awards selection committee composed of the maître d' at Elaine's, the director of admissions for the Dalton School, the senior counterman at Zabar's and the head of the co-op apartment division of Helmsley-Spear Real Estate. That agreement came after another group of Manhattan writers who insisted that they be judged only by their peers had split into warring factions over whether a writer who lives on the West Side can be considered the peer of a writer who lives on the East Side. ("If anyone can just waltz in from Amsterdam Avenue," said a novelist of manners who took the negative position, "literature has no meaning.")

As someone whose experience has been basically as a West Coast producer of television specials (the Oscar ceremonies twice, "Dumb People," "The Pope at Caesar's Palace"), Denton LaRue, the man selected to produce the Swifties, has been fairly criticized for leaning too heavily on Hollywood personalities as presenters, even though Bo Derek did handle the presentation of the poetry and translation awards with surprising good taste. Certainly there was embarrassment all around when Alan King, who arrived at the auditorium at the last minute with what turned out to have been inadequate or mistaken briefing, made it clear from his speech that he believed himself to be addressing a banquet of the Leatherwear Division of the United Jewish Appeal. After viewing last night's program, it seems less fair to criticize Mr. LaRue for recruiting dancers and singers from the entertainment industry for the large production numbers that have become his trademark at such ceremonies—although it was obviously undiplomatic of him to tell an interviewer that writers were not appropriate for such numbers because "a terminal klutziness rages rampant among them." One can only admire Norman Mailer's spunkiness in insisting that at least one writer be represented in one of the production numbers, but as the lead dancer in the "Everything Was Beautiful at the Ballet" number from *A Chorus Line,* Mr. Mailer was simply out of his depth.

This viewer came away from the set last night convinced that the organizers of the National Literary Awards had been quite unfair in characterizing as "elitist" the contention of some writers' organizations that it would be inappropriate to include in a literary awards ceremony an award for Best Catering of a Publication Party. Even if giving one award in such a field was appropriate, giving two—one for hot hors d'oeuvres and one for cold—certainly was not. All in all, the fears voiced by some writers that the ceremony's organizers would lose all restraint once they wandered away from the strictly literary seemed justified by some of the awards given last night. Was it really necessary to give an award for Best Diet Book by a Truly Fat Person? In the presence of so many authors, wasn't it just a bit insensitive to give a special publisher's award for Best Excuse for Not Advertising a Book?

Also justified, as it turns out, were the fears expressed about whether a major awards ceremony could be managed by an industry that, as Martin McCaffery said in his rather mean-spirited acceptance speech, "is pushed to the limits of its logistical capabilities trying to get ten copies of a thin novel from the warehouse to the Fifth Avenue Bren-

Cable Effect

June 7, 1980

Now that Ronald Reagan seems to have the nomination all locked up, what am I supposed to do with a leftover theory that explains why he was losing? It happens to be a perfectly good theory—a brilliant theory, really—and discarding it simply because Reagan is the only candidate left in the race seems a terrible waste in this era when we Americans are beginning to become aware of the limitations of our resources. I heard it just after the results of the Iowa caucus voting came in—around the time the political specialist NBC has analyzing these matters informed us viewers that the Reagan candidacy could virtually be written off. Reagan was losing, I was told, because of cable television: In the four years since his last attempt at the nomination, thousands of sets had been plugged into the cable system, and the reception on cable is so good that a significant proportion of the Iowa electorate was able to see exactly how old he looked.

I loved that theory. It had the simplicity of all the truly appealing political theories: Muskie lost in 1972 because he cried, Nixon lost in 1960 because his makeup ran, Ford lost in 1976 because he kept bumping his head, Humphrey lost in 1968 because the Chicago police kept bumping other people's heads. In comparison, the only other interesting explanation of Reagan's problems I heard just after the Iowa caucuses seemed hopelessly cluttered: Someone told me Reagan was defeated in Iowa because he had changed his name.

"You mean his name used to be Ronald Rabinowitz?" I said, realizing that studio heads used to force actors to shed awkward monikers.

"Of course not."

"Ronald Rigatoni? Ronald Thistlethwaite?"

"No, no."

"Ronald McDonald?"

"Don't be silly."

"Ronald Duck?"

It was explained to me that some years ago—after rather than before Reagan became an actor—he had changed the pronunciation of his name from Ree-gun to Ray-gun. According to my informant's sources, the change came with his marriage to Nancy Reagan, who, being a debutante from Chicago, did not want to sound like the wife of an Irish policeman. Chicago debutantes are particularly sensitive on that score, I was told, since most of their grandfathers were Irish policemen. The theory held that the voters of Iowa, sensing some dissonance in the presentation of Ronald Ree-gun the movie actor as Ronald Ray-gun the political candidate, rejected him for putting on airs.

I find that theory much too complicated—the way Reagan finds foreign policy. The cable television theory, on the other hand, conjures up a nice, clearly focused picture of a couple of Grant Wood farm folk up around Anamosa, which happens to be Grant Wood's hometown, settling down in front of the television to decide which candidate they're going to back at the local Republican caucus over at Center Junction, down around Onslow. The caucus is always held in conjunction with a covered-dish supper, and the folks up around Anamosa also have to face the decision of whether to bring a meatloaf or the chopped-carrot Jello mold that Walter Cronkite liked so much at the 1976 caucus.

In 1976, according to the theory, they still didn't have cable; their television reception consisted of a blurred version of the station over at Davenport, unless the wind was blowing the wrong way. They were making do with their old sixteen-inch (diagonal) black-and-white. Who needs snow in color? They were Reagan supporters. They cheered when his political commercials came on. In blurry black-and-white, Reagan still looked like The Gipper.

Then cable came. All over the country, enterprising American companies started competing to win the franchise from local authorities to bring the folks at home bright, clear pictures and a dash or two of soft porn. So much new money was changing hands that the old competitors for the attention of the City Council—real estate developers and bridge builders and insurance agents—could not get their phone calls returned from people they had been bribing for years. Sooner or later, the cable got up around Anamosa.

Pa has finished seeing to the animals, and he's settled into his favorite armchair in front of the television—a twenty-four-inch true-tone, maxi-vision color set encased in a console the size of a Dodge pickup. He is looking forward to a peaceful evening watching Robert Dole and

Phil Crane and the other fellas discuss the state of the SALT II negotiations. Ma is still in the kitchen, taking another swipe at the countertop with her ever-present sponge, and wondering whether she could get away with a double measure of bread crumbs if they decide on meatloaf for the covered-dish supper over at Center Junction.

"Ma!" Pa shouts. "Get on out here! Take a look at Ron!"

Ma bustles into the living room, wiping her hands dry on her apron. They both stare at the television set. "Land sakes alive," Ma says.

"Over by his chin there," Pa says, pointing toward the set. "It looks like the erosion over near the creek in the South Forty."

"Are those there his ears?" Ma says. "Pa, see if you can fiddle with that set just a little so's maybe his hair won't be quite that orange." The Gipper did not have orange hair.

Pa, who has always been a whiz at machinery, adjusts knobs on the television set's massive dashboard, but the candidate's hair remains orange.

"Oh my, Pa," Ma says. "Around the neck there—it looks like the chopped-carrot Jello mold."

"That does it, Ma," Pa says. "I've made up my mind. We'll take the meatloaf."

Good News at Last

June 28, 1980

Those who still do not believe there is a God in heaven have not heard the news that hot and sour soup and mushu pork may prevent heart disease. Over the past years, as tragedy and atrocity beset modern man, it has been easy to sympathize with the argument of the nonbelievers: If there is a just and merciful God and He is omnipotent, they say, how come there is so much cholesterol in Italian sausage? Why must someone who is trying to enjoy a simple plate of chopped liver be interrupted constantly by pure-food fanatics, one of whom is almost certainly his own wife, telling him that he is downing the equivalent of ground glass with schmaltz? Why has everything that tastes good been certified a killer? Now, it turns out, everything hasn't. There is a God in heaven. It is true that he may be Chinese and a bit on the enigmatic side, but He is there.

His messenger is Dr. Dale E. Hammerschmidt, a researcher at the University of Minnesota Medical School. In the *New England Journal of Medicine,* Dr. Hammerschmidt has described research leading to the theory that an ingredient common in certain Szechuan and Mandarin dishes—an ingredient called mu er or tree ears or tree fungus or black fungus—may remove fatty tissue that has built up on artery walls. Glory and Hallelujah should be said between bites of spiced Szechuan bean curd with garlic and scallions—which, as I interpret Dr. Hammerschmidt's findings, is the equivalent of penicillin that happens to taste good.

I have already dispatched a letter about Dr. Hammerschmidt to the Nobel committee. I assume they will be more responsive than they were several years ago when I tried to persuade them to award the Peace Prize to Mrs. Lisa Mosca of Mosca's restaurant in Waggaman, Louisiana, for her baked oysters. That year, they gave it to Kissinger instead.

In his journal article, Dr. Hammerschmidt wrote that he happened upon his discovery while trying to figure out why a patient's blood wasn't clotting, but I think he was being unduly modest. (Modesty was one of the attributes I mentioned in my letter to the Nobel folks.) The way I figure it, Dr. Hammerschmidt must be a man with more than a passing interest in mushu pork himself. As I imagine what must have happened, Hammerschmidt, an adventurous type, was beginning to push beyond the limits of the chop-suey joints around the campus to a couple of new Szechuan and Hunanese spots—out on what is usually referred to as the frontiers of science. Some of his more conservative colleagues—routine swallowers of egg foo young and chicken chow mein—were warning him off the best of the Szechuan restaurants merely because a professor of endocrinology happened to have keeled over there once or twice from the effects of MSG. Dr. Hammerschmidt, I figure, wanted to show up these pure-food yentas once and for all so he could enjoy his shredded spiced pork with green peppers in peace—and the rest is medical history. My tip-off was the dish he fed the control group: While his pals were feasting on the Szechuan hot bean curd, the controls were fed sweet and sour pork—a dreadful glop that is the sort of thing ordered in Chinese restaurants by my friend William Edgett Smith, the man with the Naugahyde palate.

I could hardly wait to bring the news of Dr. Hammerschmidt's discovery to my wife, Alice—who, it should be noted, has occasionally passed remarks that made it more difficult for me to enjoy a plate of chopped chicken liver, particularly if it happens to be my second or third plate. First, on the chance of acquiring the sort of independent confirmation scientists like, I went to Chinatown to see if mu er had any history as a folk medicine. In a supermarket on Mott Street, across from the amusement arcade where one can play tic-tac-toe against a live chicken, I found a package of black fungus imported from China. It said right on the package "possesses such effect as cleaning gastroenteric organs in human body"—a Chinese way of saying that a couple of bowls of hot and sour soup will make the inside of your arteries look like the finish on a brand-new Pontiac. After pausing on East Broadway for a therapeutic shot of mushu pork, I went home to tell Alice about Hammerschmidt's triumph.

"Black fungus?" she said, making it sound less than appetizing.

"Well, Aureomycin is not the sort of word I'd use in a song lyric either," I said. "What we're talking about here is wonder drugs."

"Mmmmm," she said, apparently trying to sound appropriately inscrutable.

"If you're going to bring up that time I told you that barbecue sauce improves liver function," I said, "you should keep in mind that I later admitted the theory might be somewhat premature—just a bit before all the evidence was in."

"Evidence gathered by a taxi-driver in Memphis, as I remember," Alice said.

"I trust I did not detect the sound of elitism in that last remark," I said. "The taxi-driver happened to be experienced in the area scientists call clinical application."

"Mmmmm," she said again.

"I assume you read that article I pointed out in the *Times* showing that the anti-cholesterol maniacs have been a bit premature themselves," I said, "after they spent years snatching poached eggs out of the mouths of innocent children."

"The way I read that article, there is still some dispute," she said. "Also, I couldn't find any phrase that sounded like 'the curative powers of fetuccine Alfredo.' "

I thought of showing her my package of black fungus, but I knew she would just look skeptical—the way she did when I told her fried clams might improve muscle tone. I began to feel a kinship with Hammerschmidt—facing doubters out there on the frontiers of science. It occurred to me, in fact, that the two of us might work together. Our first experiment will be to test the beneficial effects of barbecue sauce—working with a grant from the National Liver Foundation. The control group will be fed green Jello.

The Vast Wealth of Victor Navasky

July 19, 1980

When I read that Arthur Kretchmer, the editor of *Playboy,* was paid $520,734 in 1979, I began to realize what sort of money the editor of *The Nation,* one Victor Navasky, must be walking away with every year.

"I suppose Navasky's pulling down three or four hundred grand," I said to Alice, "by the time they figure in stock options and incentive bonuses and all."

"Don't be silly," she said. Could it be my imagination or is that a phrase she has begun to use more and more in my presence? Perhaps she was thinking that it hardly seems necessary to give bonuses to someone making five or ten thousand dollars a week in straight salary. I happen to know, though, that among the big bucks crowd, incentive bonuses are as common as Jaguars. I could imagine Navasky and Kretchmer and maybe the president of General Motors sitting around in some duck-hunting lodge talking about long-term capital gains and the advantages of having oneself incorporated in the Cayman Islands as a jai-lai fronton.

"Sure, people like Kretchmer and Navasky and the president of General Motors could coast along on a couple of hundred thousand all right," I told my wife. "But making those incentive bonuses is obviously a matter of pride with the heavy hitters."

"What does General Motors have to do with this?" Alice said. "General Motors makes millions of dollars. *The Nation* is always in the red."

"Maybe that's why magazines are always folding," I said. "They can't afford to pay the editors."

"Could this have something to do with that old complaint that Victor doesn't pay you enough for articles?" Alice asked. "You've been acting odd ever since that wheeler-dealer friend of yours told you that you're the labor in a labor-intensive industry."

"Not at all," I said. "It's a fact of life that the managerial class is well paid to preside over the exploitation of the workers."

But paid $520,734 a year! It is true, I told her, that the information that editors make hundreds of thousands a year permits writers to understand them a bit better. A writer who sends a manuscript to a magazine and hears nothing one way or the other for weeks has always assumed that the magazine's editor has inadvertently let the manuscript in question slip through the cracks on the porch of his beach house. We now know that it is more likely that the editor has not been able to get to the manuscript because he has to spend most of his time consulting his stockbroker or getting himself out of soybeans and into frozen hog bellies.

On the other hand, the news that editors make that much money destroyed one of my theories about the book publishing industry. I had always assumed that the reason editors in New York publishing houses spent the central three hours of their working day in fancy midtown restaurants was that the industry's standard terms of employment called for a salary of $11,500 a year plus all the overpriced French food you can eat.

"Very clever of Navasky to go around in that suit he bought while he was working for G. Mennen Williams in Michigan in 1959," I remarked to Alice one day. "I suppose this way nobody would ever think of hitting him up for a grant or a wing on the Met or anything."

"Did it ever occur to you that Arthur Kretchmer's salary at *Playboy* is not typical of editors in general?" my wife said.

I was glad she asked. I had not had the opportunity to explain a fine point of free-market economics to her since she asked me why a machine tool that some manufacturing corporation had completely depreciated over a period of ten years still exists and I told her to ask her Congressman. Only the previous week, I had been hoping that she would ask me how long and deep I thought the recession would be ("It's too early to tell" was the answer I had prepared), but she asked me instead why I never seemed to remember to wipe the kitchen counter when I'm finished with the dishes.

"Well, they've got to be in the same ballpark," I said, using a phrase I had once heard a relentlessly colloquial economist use a lot during a television interview. "Let's assume, for instance, that Arthur Kretchmer is very good at his job."

"How, precisely, would somebody be good at editing *Playboy*?" Alice asked.

"Well, let's say he's good at keeping the readers guessing all the time, not knowing what to expect next. Say they have a photo essay called 'Girls of the Sahara' one month and everybody expects something urban and sophisticated the next month—say 'Girls of the Federal Reserve System'—but he hits them with 'Girls of the Northwest Territory,' with a lot of trappers' wives and barmaids posing naked in the snow, and some of them literally frozen like ice sculpture. Hugh Hefner is delighted. He figures Kretchmer's earning every penny—$43,394.50 an issue. Even though Hefner could get Navasky or Kolatch at *The New Leader* or the fellow from *The Bulletin of the Atomic Scientists* or any number of editors for only, say, three hundred grand, he's willing to stick with Kretchmer for an extra two hundred thousand. But what if he could hire Navasky for twenty-seven five? Why, if he could hire an experienced man for even a hundred and fifty or two hundred . . ."

"I think you should quit worrying about this, and go back to work," Alice said.

I got up and walked toward my office.

"What are you going to write?" she asked.

"A letter to Hugh Hefner," I said. "I have a few ideas about his magazine that he and I should probably kick around."

Trillin as Candidate

August 30, 1980

The possibility that the Presidential election may be thrown into the House of Representatives has naturally stirred interest in the question of what sort of President Calvin Trillin would make. An examination of his record and his public statements over the years indicates that both his supporters and his critics might tend to summarize their answer to that question with the phrase "simply disastrous." The fact that a widespread assessment of that nature has not resulted in the dismissal of Mr. Trillin's candidacy has been used by some political analysts as an indication that voter dissatisfaction over the choice of Presidential candidates may run deeper than previously estimated.

There is relatively little on the public record concerning Mr. Trillin, since he has never held public office (his preference for being addressed as Governor apparently dates from a summer-camp sketch in which he played Governor Thomas E. Dewey of New York). The administrative experience suggested by the description of himself he has offered ("Administrator, Educator, Citizen-Soldier, Conspicuous Consumer") was not gathered in a governmental executive office but on the student council of Southwest High School, in Kansas City, Missouri. Although those who served on the student council with Mr. Trillin in those years tend to respond to questions about his performance in a way that suggests he was not the dominant force (the most widespread comment was "Who'd you say?"), there is simply not enough documentary evidence to enable anyone to confirm or deny the claim made for Mr. Trillin concerning his role in the council—that "he really turned it around" or that "he got it moving again."

To some extent, the same lack of documentation inhibits inquiry into Mr. Trillin's experience as an educator—his service on the parents' committee of P.S. 3, a public elementary school in lower Manhattan. It is impossible to confirm that the year of Mr. Trillin's service saw "a complete reorganization of the recess safety program," or, if so, whether Mr. Trillin was significantly involved in that project. Memories of such committee meetings are, of course, selective and unreliable—as demonstrated by the committee chairman's description of Mr. Trillin recently as "the one who usually hit the wine and cheese table pretty hard."

Little is known about the sort of person who might be chosen to fill a major post in a Trillin Administration. When asked some time ago about whom he depended on for advice on foreign affairs, Mr. Trillin mentioned Paul Adler, of New York, who turned out to be his travel agent. Although Mr. Adler is widely respected in his field, he has expressed no interest in leaving his business to accept a position in government. Reporters who ask Mr. Trillin whose advice he seeks in military matters are given the name of Patrick J. Powers, formerly of Chicago. In the late 1950s, Mr. Powers and Mr. Trillin were fellow enlisted men at First United States Army Headquarters on Governors Island, in New York Harbor, where Mr. Powers was widely respected for attributes that included the quality of the spit shine on his Army boots. (This was the period during which Mr. Trillin participated in the engagement alluded to in the phrase "gun-toting" citizen-soldier: In a platoon-in-the-attack demonstration for Armed Forces Day Open House, he was among those soldiers who landed in a helicopter flown from Staten Island, swept down the airfield and captured the incinerator from a detachment of computer operators.) Mr. Powers retired several years ago with the rank of Master Sergeant. It is difficult to ascertain where he stands on some of the military issues that might come before a President, since he has made no public statements himself and Mr. Trillin remains vague about the policy implications of the quotation he often credits to Mr. Powers—"a place for everything, everything in its place."

Not having ever served as a legislator—the claims that he was some sort of dormitory representative in college seem to have been withdrawn—Mr. Trillin has no legislative record that might offer clues to the sort of policies his Administration would pursue. His voting record in regular elections is, by general agreement, unusual—what he calls "independent" and his critics have characterized as "off the wall." He has acknowledged in print that he voted for John V. Lindsay in one mayoral race simply because Mr. Lindsay's wife had responded to being restricted to the women's balcony of an annual New York political dinner by flicking peanuts on those beneath her. Yet, in 1972, he refused to back Mr. Lindsay in his bid for the Democratic Presidential nomination—and for reasons some observers

The Plastic Surgery Issue

September 27, 1980

Although a full week has passed since First Lady Nancy Reagan resumed her regular schedule, the White House remains unsuccessful in its efforts to still rumors that the cause of her brief absence was an operation for the surgical removal of her adoring smile.

Officially, the White House has not even acknowledged that Mrs. Reagan's apparent inability to look at her husband with any expression other than an adoring smile may have caused the President some embarrassment at official functions that called for a certain solemnity—most recently at his announcement that Social Security checks would henceforth be sent only to those Americans who had reached what he described as "the more realistic retirement age" of 82.

Such comments began to find their way into print last fall, when President Reagan made his long-awaited announcement on how he intended to increase defense spending and reduce income taxes at the same time—announcing a plan that, shorn of its rhetoric, seemed to be little more than that old conservative-Republican chestnut of an "across-the-board bread tax." Some reporters interpreted the smile Mrs. Reagan wore while the President proposed a "disincentive surcharge" on day-old bread as reflecting a lack of sympathy for the poor.

Barely a month later, when the President and Mrs. Reagan flew to Jidda for the funeral of the Saudi Prime Minister, most foreign affairs analysts concluded that whatever diplomatic gain was realized by the gesture was probably offset by the widely distributed photo of the First Lady beaming amid a clot of wailing Arab women as the President delivered a eulogy. The criticism was summed up by the semiofficial Jordanian daily *El Shri,* which said in a lead editorial that Mrs. Reagan's adoring smile was "the best argument we in the Moslem world have seen for the reinstitution of the veil."

At the time, President Reagan was able to brush aside a press conference question about the First Lady's smile by recalling the film debut of the song "Let a Smile Be Your Umbrella" and telling several anecdotes about Gene Kelly's antics on Hollywood sets. He had the confidence that might have been expected from someone who, alone among modern Presidents, seemed to be remarkably free of embarrassments caused by family members. A strong desire to avoid such embarrassments rather than any coldness in the family has been offered privately by Presidential aides as the reason President and Mrs. Reagan have not yet invited any of their children to the White House. The closest thing to a family flap the Administration has undergone was the quickly forgotten NBC interview with two freelance photographers who said there was reason to believe that the President's younger son, Ron, did not in fact know his father when he saw him—the photographers having been stalking Ron on Fifth Avenue when he shouted "Hiya

Dad!" to a man who turned out to be Joel McCrea.

Although President Reagan can still deal from strength where his family's behavior is concerned, the First Lady's absence has reopened a question potentially much more dangerous: In the sense that the Nixon Administration was overwhelmed by Watergate, and the Johnson Administration was undermined by Vietnam, has the Reagan Administration been thrown off balance by its multifaceted connection with plastic surgery? During the campaign, Mr. Reagan vigorously denied suggestions that he himself had undergone some cosmetic facial surgery; most observers here think that the country had come to believe Mr. Reagan's denials, and that he was badly advised to repeat them in his first State of the Union Address. Within weeks, there was a mild controversy about his choosing as Surgeon General a physician who had once been known as "The Tummy Tuck King of Palm Beach." Still, the matter might have faded from public memory if the President had not startled his conservative followers with his support of a policy permitting welfare recipients to receive face-lifts on Medicaid.

Now, reporters are again asking questions about plastic surgery. Why, they want to know, has the only *amicus curiae* brief filed by the Civil Rights Division of the Justice Department been in defense of the plastic surgeon appealing the judgment awarded against him in the so-called Misplaced Belly Button Case? Why has Betty Ford, who has openly spoken of her face-lift, been at the White House for so many state functions to which her husband, the former President, was not invited?

The President's supporters maintain that the liberal press,

desperate to find a weak spot in the Simple Deal program of the Reagan Administration, has been irresponsible and even libelous. It is true that, whether *The New York Times* wishes to call its later version of the events a correction or a "further refinement," no one can now say for certain that a nurse present during Vice President George Bush's annual physical examination definitely overheard Mr. Bush ask the attending physicians if something might be done to make him look "a little less preppie around the eyes."

The question the White House has not been able to answer satisfactorily, though, is why Mrs. Reagan has not smiled adoringly at the President since her return; if she did indeed have a Novocain injection during some dental work, it should have worn off by now. There is now speculation in Washington—based on no known scientific evidence—that the surgical removal of a smile, if it indeed took place, might have led to an overall change in attitude. There could be any number of explanations for the fact that the First Lady emitted a sigh during last Tuesday's White House ceremony for the National Association of Manufacturers' Depreciator of the Year, at about the time the President was repeating his familiar story about how many people General Motors had to employ to fill out Government forms. It is indicative of White House sensitivity on the entire subject that it chose to release a fourteen-page white paper on the incident, and to furnish affidavits denying that the First Lady turned to the person on her right and said, "If I have to listen to that story one more time I'll simply collapse."

Sukey as First Sister

October 18, 1980

What I've been most worried about lately is whether my sister, Sukey, would do something to embarrass me if I became President. I realize, of course, that there are people who believe that I have no serious chance at the Presidency, at least this time around. It is true that the rumor that buoyed the spirits of my supporters for a while—the rumor that a columnist on an established Midwestern weekly, the *Thursday Shopper* of Raytown, Missouri, planned to refer to me in his column as a "spoiler"—turned out to be premature. Since then, I'll admit, I have more or less stopped active campaigning, although I still pass a cutting remark about Phil Crane now and then just to keep in practice. Also, I have not abandoned the official complaint I filed with the Fair Campaign Practices Committee many months ago accusing John B. Connally of "unfair hair." I intend to see that one through. Still, I would be the first to admit that I'm a long shot.

The way I figure it, though, this is precisely the time to grapple with matters such as the embarrassment potential of my family and whether someone could make an issue out of past personal remarks made to me by my banker in the course of business ("Pull up your socks, Trillin!") and how one goes about arranging to have certain records of the Kansas City Board of Education destroyed without a trace. If a time comes when the Presidential nomination of a major party seems within my grasp, reporters will be swarming over Kansas City and the surrounding countryside to poke around at my family and my early years—nipping over to Topeka to see which word my Cousin Keith from Salina missed in the finals of the Kansas State Spelling Bee ("hayseed"), driving up to St. Jo to go through the police reports on the time my Uncle Benny Daynofsky was struck down by a Pontiac GTO while planting tomatoes in his back yard, visiting Lincoln to make certain that there were no election irregularities when my Cousin Neil was chosen head drum major of the University of Nebraska marching band, pumping old school chums to see if they happen to have saved some embarrassing souvenir like a Halloween picture of me costumed as Eleanor of Aquitaine, trying to get the goods on my sister, Sukey.

If I made any attempt at that time to counsel old friends about putting certain incidents into perspective ("Sure, it was the funniest thing that happened all eighth-grade year, Eddie, but if you told that story to people who don't happen to understand the traditional place of farm animals in the humor of this region the way you and I do, well, there just might be some misunderstanding . . ."), some of those post-Watergate snoops would be certain to accuse me of trying to tidy up my background for campaign purposes. Even at this early date, some of them might read some fence-mending motives into the fact that I just dedicated a book to my sister—especially if they find out that the dedication originally read, "To my sister, Sukey Fox, in a first tentative step toward forgiving her for trying to throw me down the laundry chute in 1937."

Was I being overcautious? On the surface, after all, Sukey seems respectable enough. She has been married for twenty-five years to the same husband. She has raised three unindicted sons. It is true that she is a real estate agent, an occupation that the public tends to rank in trustworthiness only slightly higher than journalist, but her inability to overcome a lifelong compulsion toward total disclosure makes her one of those rare real estate agents who might inform the prospective buyers of the Cape Colonial Split-Level Ranch that the odd pinging noise from the cellar does indeed sound like a boiler self-destructing. Could I cast doubt on the patriotism of someone who has borne witness to some twenty-three hundred hours of Little League play? Did I think there was any chance of alcohol abuse by someone whose intake of strong drink is limited to a chocolate-marshmallow daiquiri every other New Year's Eve?

On the other hand, who can predict how someone will react to temptation? Sure, Sukey seems O.K. now, but the way I read Billy Carter's testimony he was a model citizen himself until the voters went and ruined his life by making his brother President. It may be that if Helen Gahagan Douglas had successfully countered her opponent's accusations that she was an agent of the Red Menace, Donald Nixon would now be a solvent and contented insurance adjuster in Anaheim, California. What if Sukey started getting offers to appear at shopping center openings and trade smart remarks with Bobby Riggs and Debbie Reynolds and Annette Funicello and that crowd? What if she started getting nibbles from *Hollywood Squares* and *Card Sharks?* How many of us could keep our heads under those circumstances? As it happens, Sukey has some time on her hands these days. Her youngest son, Stevie, left for college last year. (Stevie! Could it be that Stevie, forgetting all the Lego blocks I lavished on him, will embarrass me by organizing panty raids at the University of Kansas?) The real estate game is slow, now that the only way to get mortgage money from a bank is to stage a successful armed robbery. What if Sukey met some Libyans? What if Sukey met some Libyans with mortgage money? Before you know it, the pack would be after us. Sukeygate.

The shuttle shrinks would analyze the entire business in terms of Sukey's subsconscious need to lash out—as Donald Nixon and Billy Carter lashed out—at an older brother who had picked on her as a child. Wait a minute! I'm her younger brother. I didn't try to throw her down the laundry chute; she tried to throw me down the laundry chute. Suddenly encouraged, I phoned Sukey in Kansas City.

"You wouldn't embarrass me if I became President, would you Sukey?" I said, when she answered.

There was silence for a while on the other end of the line. Finally, Sukey said, "Sometimes I'm sorry you were too fat."

"Too fat to be President?"

"Too fat to fit down the laundry chute."

Unhealth Food

November 8, 1980

"Am I the only one worried about how unhealthy the people who work in health food stores look?" I said to my wife, Alice, one day. I described, in some detail, a clerk I had just encountered in a health food store—his sunken chest, his quivering hands, his ominous pallor, the dun-colored tint to his wretched little wispy beard.

"Calm down," Alice said.

"Why isn't there a Whole Grain Defense Committee working to put some meat on their bones?" I said. "I'm beginning to think those Washington soothsayers are right about how uncaring Americans have become. Dozens of customers a day must walk right by this quasi cadaver and not one of them is willing to get involved even to the extent of calling 911."

"What were you doing in a health food store anyway?" Alice asked. "You're always saying that health food makes you sick."

"I was on a mission of mercy," I said. "A friend of mine who lives in a place that lacks the shopping resources of this great city had run out of soy waste."

"You know very well there's no such thing as soy

waste," she said. "Why do you keep going on about soy waste?"

"Soy waste, granola dust, pure extract of balsa wood—what's the difference what they call it?" I said. "Judging from the condition of the clerk, it obviously isn't enough to keep a human being alive."

It happens to be true that health food makes me sick. In fact, health food stores make me feel a bit queasy even if I don't buy anything—partly, I think, because they always smell like capsules that have been in the medicine chest since the Nixon-Humphrey campaign.

"The children said you made a scene in the store," Alice said.

"Not a scene, really," I said. It is true that, as I poked around the aisles looking for the soy waste, I stopped to sniff the air, and suddenly heard myself shout, "Help! I'm trapped in a bottle of Coricidin!" That isn't really a scene though. I think of it as more of an outburst.

"I think you're becoming a crank," Alice said.

"This is pure science we're talking about here," I said. "If bumblebee leavings and stump paste are so good for you, why can't any of those guys grow full beards? Isn't there some public health law against people who are shopping for food being reminded constantly of the last days of Howard Hughes? These health food store people look even less healthy than runners."

"What do runners have to do with this?" Alice asked.

"Plenty," I said. "I'm glad you brought it up. Did you get a look at those guys who ran in the New York Marathon? They look like they make their living as male models for refugee relief ads: 'You can either send this lunatic a Mars bar or you can turn the page.' "

"I see now that this is not crankiness," Alice said.

"Support from home is always welcome," I said. "Even if it comes a bit late."

"What it is," she went on, "is a devious attempt to justify a style of life that is based on sausage-eating and sloth."

"Which reminds me," I said. "Am I the only person who favors a law mandating life imprisonment for anyone who performs in public as a mime? Where is everybody else on these issues?"

"Don't try to change the subject," she said.

"Who's changing the subject? I've been talking about this for years." It happens to be true that it has been several years since I pointed out to Alice that everybody in the world—way down deep—has a response to mimes that is reflected in the Woody Allen line about watching a mime who was "either blowing glass or tattooing the student body of Northwestern University." Certainly, my early commitment to the cause was demonstrated to anyone's satisfaction in 1978 when I attempted to place some mimes who were performing in Sheridan Square under citizen's arrest.

"Picking on mimes has—"

"I hope you're not going to drag out that tiresome business about the First Amendment," I said. "It is perfectly obvious that the right of free speech has been waived, de facto, by people who have a policy of not saying anything."

"I gather from this conversation that you suspect I might have discovered the gumbo with andouille sausage you smuggled in from Louisiana and hid in the freezer," Alice said.

"And speaking of border crossings," I said. "Who is it in the State Department who persists in granting visas to Marcel Marceau—a man who advertises in the newspaper that he intends to commit middlebrow felonies all over the country?"

"You're simply going to have to control your eating," she said. "I promised your mother I would—"

"I suppose you're going to bring up the fact that October 26 was Mother-in-Laws' Day," I said. "A testimony to the imagination of the American cut-flowers industry. I assume they'll be having Landlords' Day next—some date at the end of a cold month, when most evictions occur. Then Life Insurance Salesmen's Day."

"Also, a little exercise wouldn't do you any harm."

"Customs Inspectors' Day," I said. "Then a day for sending posies to the hard-working folks who dun you for your Diners Club bill."

"I think you should throw out the gumbo right now," Alice said.

"Am I the only one who thinks foreign movies are for sissies or are the others just not saying?" I said.

"I take back what I said about crankiness," Alice said.

"Thank you."

"You are, in fact, a crank," she said. "A sausage-eating, slothful crank."

Mary knows otherwise. She used to go to birthday parties at the mansion when she herself was a student at Girls Latin. The *Playboy* mansion was then owned by a prominent Chicago physician who kept monkeys. I wish I could report that the doctor/monkey keeper was Nancy Reagan's stepfather, Dr. Loyal Davis. My source tells me otherwise. I wish I could at least report that Nancy Reagan herself attended birthday parties at the *Playboy* mansion—sitting primly with her ice cream and cake in what was to become the steam room where Art Buchwald, his glasses fogged over, mistook Shel Silverstein for Miss South Dakota. I can't be sure of that, though, because Nancy Reagan is—if I may say so without provoking an audit of my taxes or a short spell of preventive detention—quite a bit older than Mary. What I am sure of—sure enough to print—is that Nancy Reagan was known as Bubbles at Girls Latin.

Of course, I could double-check the story by phoning Mary's mother, who still lives in Chicago. Fortunately, I have had enough experience in the reporting game to avoid that trap. Twenty years ago, when the better restaurants of Atlanta were segregated by law but wary of offending the occasional foreign dignitary who happened to be dark-complected, I heard that a black woman who taught drama at Clark College was able to dine regularly with her white friends at the fanciest French restaurant in town by wearing a turban and speaking Spanish. I used to treasure the vision of the drama teacher sitting imperiously at the head of the table, criticizing the service in high school Spanish whenever a waiter came within earshot. I used to treasure the vision of the elegantly dressed headwater explaining what was going on to a puzzled, if equally sophisticated-looking, sommelier ("Ah guess she's one of them furriners, Luke"). I used to enjoy speculating about which country the restaurant's proprietor thought a black woman wearing a turban and speaking Spanish came from. Then, just before I was about to reveal this situation to the world—using one of reporting's old standby phrases like "It is said that . . ." or "People here tell the story of . . ."—I made the mistake of checking on whether the story was true. What I found out was that the drama teacher had never been to the restaurant and that I therefore could not use the story. What I learned was a lesson that some people in the field have suggested as a motto for the Columbia University Graduate School of Journalism—"What you don't know can't hurt you," or, as it has been translated from the Latin by Philosopher of Journalism Richard Cohen, "The best stories never check out." I am absolutely certain that Mary's mother would confirm her story, but why take a chance?

Now that I have broken the Bubbles story, will my colleagues in the press follow my lead? Their performance after my last exclusive about the Reagan family does not engender confidence. Last June—when the Washington press corps, in a display of the "pack journalism" we have heard so much about, seemed stuck on such questions as whether Ronald Reagan's approach to foreign policy might result in the annihilation of human society as we know it—I revealed that Reagan used to be pronounced Ree-gun rather than Ray-gun. I assumed that the reporters of the Washington pack would be after that one with the joyous yelps for which they are known in certain Capitol Hill saloons. I had already done most of the digging for them, after all—even to the point of raising the possibility that the name-change had been made at the behest of Nancy Reagan, a proper Chicago debutante who obviously wanted to avoid sounding Irish because of all the dirty stuff in *Studs Lonigan*.

My colleagues have still hardly mentioned the name-change to Ray-gun. Can they continue to ignore the story after this latest bombshell? It is now possible, after all, that the woman we know as Nancy Ray-gun is, in fact, Bubbles Ree-gun. How are we expected to reconcile that with the picture of Nancy Ray-gun the press has drawn? Is it really possible that a woman who was once—even for a day—called Bubbles always smiles and never giggles? Could the Nancy Reagan we know have really had the same childhood nickname as Beverly Sills? Impossible? In that case, could it be that the woman we know as Nancy Ray-gun is not the former Bubbles Davis who attended Girls Latin School? But why would Ronald Reagan's wife want to pretend she was somebody she wasn't? Why indeed! Didn't somebody just write a novel about a President's wife being a foreign agent? We must face the possibility that the woman who calls herself Nancy Ray-gun is what the folks in the spy game call a mole—a mole with a fixed smile, but still a mole. The implication is not simply that our next President might find himself snoring away next to an agent of the Kremlin. The implication is this: If the Russians knew enough to establish an agent-in-place among the starlets on the MGM lot in 1944, they know a lot more about us than we thought they knew.

Dinner at the de la Rentas'

January 17, 1981

Another week has passed without my being invited to the de la Rentas'. Even that overstates my standing. Until I read in *The New York Times Magazine* a couple of weeks ago about the de la Rentas having become ''barometers of what constitutes fashionable society'' (''Françoise and Oscar de la Renta have created a latter-day salon for *le nouveau grand monde*—the very rich, very powerful and very gifted''), I wasn't even aware of what I wasn't being invited to week after week. Once I knew, of course, it hurt.

Every time the phone rang, I thought it might be Mrs. de la Renta with an invitation (''Mr. Trillin? Françoise de la Renta here. We're having a few very rich, very powerful and/or very gifted people over Sunday evening to celebrate Tisha B'av, and we thought you and the missus might like to join us''). The phone rang. It was the lady from the Diners' Club informing me how quickly a person's credit rating can deteriorate. The phone rang. It was my mother calling from Kansas City to ask if I'm sure I sent a thank-you note to my Cousin Edna for the place setting of stainless Edna and six other cousins went in on for our wedding gift in 1965. The phone rang. An invitation! Fats Goldberg, the pizza baron, asked if we'd like to bring the kids to his uptown branch Sunday night to sample the sort of pizza he regularly describes as "a gourmet tap-dance."

"Thanks, Fat Person, but I'll have to phone you," I said. "We may have another engagement Sunday."

The phone quit ringing.

"Why aren't I in *le nouveau grand monde?*" I asked my wife, Alice.

"Because you speak French with a Kansas City accent?" she asked in return.

"Not at all," I said. "Sam Spiegel, the Hollywood producer, is a regular at the de la Rentas', and I hear that the last time someone asked him to speak French he said 'Gucci.' "

"Why would you want to go there anyway?" Alice said. "Didn't you read that the host is so phony he added his own 'de la' to what had been plain old Oscar Renta?"

"Who can blame a man for not wanting to go through life sounding like a taxi driver?" I said. "Family background's not important in *le nouveau grand monde*. Diana Vreeland says Henry Kissinger is the star. The Vicomtesse de Ribes says 'Françoise worships intelligence.' You get invited by accomplishment—taking over a perfume company, maybe, or invading Cambodia."

"Why don't we just call Fats and tell him we'll be there for a gourmet tap-dance?" Alice said.

"Maybe it would help if you started wearing dresses designed by Oscar de la Renta," I said. "Some of his guests say they would feel disloyal downing Mrs. d's chicken fricassee while wearing someone else's merchandise."

Alice shook her head. "Oscar de la Renta designs those ruffly dresses that look like what the fat girl made a bad mistake wearing to the prom," she said.

"Things were a lot easier when fashionable society was limited to old-rich goyim, and all the rest of us didn't have to worry about being individually rejected," I said.

"At least they knew better than to mingle socially with their dressmakers," Alice said.

Would I be ready if the de la Rentas phoned? The novelist Jerzy Kosinski, after all, told the *Times* that evenings with them were "intellectually demanding." Henry Kissinger, the star himself, said that the de la Rentas set "an interesting intellectual standard"—although, come to think of it, that phrase could also be applied to Fats Goldberg.

Alone at the kitchen table, I began to polish my dinner-table chitchat, looking first to the person I imagined being seated on my left (the Vicomtesse de Ribes, who finds it charming that her name reminds me of barbecue joints in Kansas City) and then to the person on my right (Barbara Walters, another regular, who has tried to put me at my ease by confessing that in French she doesn't do her r's terribly well). "I was encouraged when it leaked that the Reagan Cabinet was going to be made up of successful managers from the world of business," I say, "but I expected them all to be Japanese."

Barbara and the Vicomtesse smile. Alice, who had just walked into the kitchen, looked concerned.

"Listen," Alice said. "I read in the *Times* that Mrs. de la Renta is very strict about having only one of each sort of person at a dinner party. Maybe they already have someone from Kansas City."

Possible. Jerzy Kosinski mentioned that Mrs. d is so careful about not including more than one stunning achiever from each walk of life ("she understands that every profession generates a few princes or kings") that he and Norman Mailer have never been at the de la Rentas' on the same evening ("when I arrive, I like to think that, as a novelist, I'm unique"). Only one fabulous beauty. Only one world-class clotheshorse.

Then I realized that the one-of-each rule could work to my advantage. As I envisioned it, Henry Kissinger phones Mrs. d only an hour before dinner guests are to arrive. He had been scheduled to pick up fifteen grand that night for explaining SALT II to the Vinyl Manufacturers Association convention in Chicago, but the airports are snowed in. He and Nancy will be able to come to dinner after all. "How marvelous, darling!" Mrs. d says.

She hangs up and suddenly looks stricken. "My God!" she says to Oscar. "What are we going to do? We already have one war criminal coming!"

What to do except to phone the man who conflicts with the star and tell him the dinner had to be called off because Mr. d had come down with a painful skin disease known as the Seventh Avenue Shpilkes. What to do about the one male place at the table now empty—between Vicomtesse de Ribes and Barbara Walters?

The phone rings. "This is Françoise de la Renta," the voice says.

"This is Calvin of the Trillin," I say. "I'll be right over."

Understanding Preppies

February 7, 1981

My initial response to the appearance of *The Official Preppy Handbook,* now a paperback best seller, was quite simple: I don't need any preppies to tell me about preppies, thank you very much. As Frank Boyden, the legendary headmaster of the Deerfield School, said upon his retirement after eighty-nine years at the helm, "I know from preppies already." Lists of appropriate names for heirs and cutesy nicknames for debutantes are not enlightening to someone whose freshman roommate in college—a quarter of a century ago—had three last names and a sister called Caca. To quote what Dr. Boyden had to say on an entirely different matter (the signing of the Declaration of Independence), "I vas dere, Sharlie."

All of the basic research on this subject was completed by the middle fifties in New Haven, Connecticut—most of it by me. We didn't use the word "preppy" then, of course. That word was more or less invented in 1970 by Erich Segal in *Love Story,* the novel in which Segal also popularized the phrase "Love is not having to call me a schlockmeister." We didn't have a word for preppies at all; there were too many to call anything. In those days, someone in New Haven who wanted to study preppyism found himself in the position of a tax-shelter salesman at a medical convention: the prospects were thick on the ground.

My most intense observation, though, was of my roommate, Thatcher Baxter Hatcher (nickname: Tush) and his sister—whose real name, of course, was not Caca but Baxter Thatcher Hatcher. Tush and Caca were completely open about answering my questions, even those that might have been brushed aside as too personal by people not as carefully brought up to be courteous ("If you folks are so rich, Tush, why don't any of you have a first name?"). They reminded me of those Hottentots I had seen in *National Geographic* joking and making faces while a clutch of anthropologists poked around at their rib cages and put calipers to their craniums. Of course, misunderstandings are always possible in the area of research that historians and scientists usually footnote as "personal communication." When Tush informed me, for instance, that after the war (Second World) his family no longer bothered to dress for dinner every evening, I thought he meant that they ate in their underwear ("My mom'd never let us come to the table like that, Tush, and I'm talking about Kansas City").

Tush's openness, though, soon led to my breakthrough on the origin of the characteristic preppy accent: I realized that he was being closemouthed about his background only in the sense that his mouth was almost literally closed. He didn't seem to need to open it to talk. After some attempt at amateur speech therapy ("Tush, you're going to have to round out those vowels a little, old guy; you sound like someone who just ate his way out of a case of Skippy chunk-style") and a few attempts to josh him out of it ("Tush, old buddy, I don't mind you imitating a ventriloquist, but does your dummy have to speak Latvian?''), I began some investigations which led to the discovery that at the age of twelve every boy at St. Paul's School or Groton has his jaw broken with one clean stroke of a wooden mallet wielded by a man whose previous job was stunning the cattle at the Kansas City stockyards just before they are dispatched. I left it to other researchers to divine the significance, if any, in the fact that twelve is precisely the age at which every Hottentot boy has his ear lobes lowered and ''Mom'' tattooed on his left forearm.

I was also the investigator who did all of the basic work on preppy taste in food—having completed, by 1957, most of the research involved in what is now routinely referred to as the White Bread Effect. The breakthrough in this case came during a wedding reception at the Piping Rock Club, on the north shore of Long Island, when, in an effort to compliment the mother of the bride on the spread she had arranged to have put before us, I said, ''Mrs. Thatcher, the Velveeta cheese slices on pieces of quartered day-old Wonder Bread are absolutely marvelous.'' It was at that moment that I put together the theory that became the underpinning of the White Bread Effect: At American weddings, the quality of the food is in inverse proportion to the social position of the bride and groom.

As I grumbled recently about the handbookists of the moment having arrived at the study of *prepismo* rather late in the game, I realized that I was surprised that the game was still going on. I had always assumed that after the era that scholars refer to as The Golden Age of Preppies (circa 1953–57), the number of preppies around gradually diminished as the admission offices of established Eastern colleges gradually put themselves at risk to the perils of democracy. I don't mean that I thought preppies had become extinct—I run into old Tush Hatcher now and then when he takes his son, young Tushie, to midtown for his mumbling lessons—but I assumed the preppy population was considerably reduced in size and influence, like the population of panda bears or officers of the British Colonial Service.

Wrong again. There seem to be more preppies than ever. There are more people who want to consider themselves preppies even though they are not properly placed in the subspecies St. Grottlesex—furriers' sons who go to day school in the Bronx, crackers named Billy Joe who attended the second oldest seg academy in Waycross, Georgia. The garment sharks fob off crew-neck sweaters on Irish secretaries as part of the preppy look. Is some natural law at work—the same natural law under which fifty years of tax reform has produced more millionaires who don't pay taxes than there ever were before?

Preppies are back. I read in the Inauguration coverage that chincilla coats and ten-thousand-dollar ball gowns are also back. Will everything now come back? Child labor? The Spanish-American War? Could this be what Ronald Reagans means by a new beginning? Will all of us have to eat Velveeta on stale Wonder Bread at wedding receptions?

The President as Dingbat

February 28, 1981

"Daddy, why is there a picture of the President's handwriting in *The New York Times*?"

"The White House wants to demonstrate that the President can, in fact, read and write. It makes the citizens feel more secure. Also, it's good for what they call 'reassuring our allies.' What kind of cereal do you want for breakfast—the stuff with a year's supply of thiamine hydrochloride or the stuff that has enough riboflavin to give you an out-of-body experience?"

"What do you mean about a picture of the President's handwriting reassuring our allies, Daddy?"

"Well, sometimes people like the French and the English and the Germans worry about the person who's President of the United States not being too bright—particularly since that state dinner in Paris when President Ford ate the centerpiece. They seem to think that a President who's not too bright might push the wrong button and incinerate Bulgaria or someplace and cause a lot of trouble for everyone."

"Daddy, Mommy says that if you never give me a straight answer I might grow up to be a smart aleck like you."

"All right. If you must know, the picture is supposed

to demonstrate that the President wrote the first draft of his television speech all by himself—unless he copied it from an old Calvin Coolidge speech he found stuck back in one of the drawers in the White House. You see, some people keep saying that the President is just an actor who says whatever the people around him tell him to say, and, since the people around him are these rich old guys from California who own car dealerships and drugstore chains, if it isn't shown that he sometimes writes his own speeches people might worry that just when everyone expects him to talk about something like the State of the Union he'll start hawking Ford Fairlanes or announcing a special, for this week only, on hair spray."

"Do you mean that the President is a retard?"

"If you happen to meet the French or English ambassadors, I really think it would be better not to use that word. It might upset them."

"But Daddy, there's a spelling mistake in his first sentence."

"Nobody's perfect."

" 'Tonight' isn't spelled t-o-n-i-t-e."

"Well, it's very close. Many of the same letters. I'd like to come to the President's defense on that one."

"Why are you defending him—just because you always have to ask Mommy how to spell 'occurred'?"

"No, I am defending him because I give each President one free defense in the first month of his Administration, followed by three years and eleven months of underhanded, mean-spirited abuse. It's what I've tried to teach you about fair play."

"I don't think that's really a very good defense—that a lot of the letters are the same. Do you?"

"Well, 'tonight' is sometimes spelled that way on cue-cards. Also in advertisements—like 'Test the new Fairlane at our Long Beach or San Pedro showroom, both open till nine tonite.' "

"But Daddy, 'tonite' means a high explosive compound of pulverized guncotton impregnated with barium nitrate."

"What are you reading that from?"

"The *Oxford English Dictionary.*"

"Well, that definition is another little something I wouldn't mention to the French or English ambassadors. Could you just check the spelling of 'occurred,' by the way, as long as you have the book right there?"

"I really think the President should be able to spell."

"We're living in an era of limited expectations."

"Can the Vice President spell?"

"I have it on good authority that the Vice President is an excellent speller. Our friend John Cole says he used to sneak looks at the Vice President's paper during exams at Yale, and he was quite impressed with the Vice President's spelling. Also his handwriting. Very legible, John says, even from a distance. I think we can be reassured on that point. There's a first-rate speller right in the White House inner circle."

"The President left some commas out in the second sentence. We get marked down for leaving out commas."

"Look, let's get this in perspective. Punctuation and spelling aren't everything. If you put this in perspective, it isn't even so terrible that the man the President nominated for Deputy Secretary of State couldn't name the Prime Minister of South Africa.''

''You mean they gave him a quiz? How many did he get right?''

''He didn't get any right.''

''So what did they do to him?''

''They made him Deputy Secretary of State.''

''We get marked down for not getting any right.''

''Well, there's a feeling that the President ought to have his own team in there with him.''

''What do they call the team—the Slow Learners?''

''I do think you're getting to be a smart aleck. It must be all that riboflavin.''

''So go ahead and put it all in perspective.''

''Well, you see, the President wants efficient people like successful corporate executives on his team. Corporate executives don't need to spell or remember names; they have secretaries to do that. The Deputy Secretary of State would just say to his secretary, ''Honey, get me the guy in charge of that big country at the bottom of Africa—the one where the coloreds are always causing trouble.'' Also, if you put this spelling business into even more perspective, simplified spelling like t-o-n-i-t-e is consistent with the President's approach to government. He says that the Federal Government has become much too complicated. The President wants everything to be simpler.''

''So do the slow learners in my class.''

Country Sounds

March 21, 1981

I was standing in a supermarket checkout line not long ago when I thought of a new Country & Western single: "It's No Wonder Your Hair's Always in Curlers 'Cause You've Never Been Straight With Me." It just came to me. A lot of Country & Western songs had been coming to me. I thought I knew where they came from: The tipoff was that they were, without exception, dreadful Country & Western songs. Once, I had made up a character in a book who thought up truly awful Country & Western songs—Duane Minnick, a gas-station attendant who wrote "The Coveralls I Wear May Be Green But I'm the Bluest Car Mechanic You Ever Seen" and "I'm Just a Loaner While You Wait for the Two-Door Hardtop of Your Dreams" ("You used to be here, but right now you're there./ You done left me for chrome and factory air"). I figured that for reasons I couldn't imagine—my behavior since the book had been impeccable—Minnick had come back to live inside me, like some sullen grease-stained sprite. There was a time when seeing a lot of women wearing curlers at the supermarket would have just made me think that maybe we were in for a prom, or maybe the President had asked everyone to wear curlers until the Japanese quit dumping color televisions sets on the American market. It was the presence of Minnick, I figured, that caused the sight to put lyrics in my head:

> You can't hear me 'cause you're still under the dryer.
> So I'm saying that you're nothing but a frizzy-haired liar.
> Some day, when you're standing there combing it out,
> I'm going to put down my own blow-dryer and shout,
> "It's no wonder your hair's always in curlers 'cause you've never been straight with me."

For a while, I thought the songs were brought on by being in what might be considered country music settings—what New York social scientists refer to in their monographs as "places where you find a lot of schleppers." After all, I had been in an electronic games arcade when I wrote "You Shot Me Down in the Electronic Game of Life":

> You tell me you found another and you wouldn't trade her
> For two hundred points on Space Invaders.
> It's all so cruel; it's so downright mean.
> I'm nothing but a blip on your Atari machine.

Then, I happened to be watching the television coverage of a Senate hearing that seemed to be held to determine whether President Reagan's nominee for Deputy Secretary of State knew less about foreign policy than President Reagan's nominee for Secretary of Energy knew about energy. According to my information, these hearings took place in order to settle some betting on the subject that had been going on in the Senate cloakroom, back behind the windbreakers. The winners, by the way, turned out to be the Senators who had put their money on the unalloyed ignorance of the new man at State: The Energy Secretary, a dental surgeon before he entered politics, marred an otherwise perfect record by informing the Senators of the precise energy costs involved in the simple removal of an abscess from the gum.

When the man nominated to be Deputy Secretary of State was asked some question to test his knowledge of world affairs—as I remember, he was asked whether the monarch of the United Kingdom is Queen Elizabeth II or the Baal Shem Tov—he knit his brow in concentration, and I, instead of blurting out the answer in order to impress my children, found myself singing a C&W single called "I Was Your Double-Knit Lover But We're Both Single Again":

> You used to say you'd never seen nothing quite so cute
> As me in my salmon-pink leisure suit.
> And now you leave my heart to dry up and crack and fester.
> To you, I'm just a used-up old pile of polyester.
> I was your double-knit lover, but we're both single again.

Could it really have been, I asked myself, that "double-knit" came from watching the future administrator of the State Department knit his brow? That would have been a pretty subtle play on words for an ignorant grease monkey like Duane Minnick. Would alliteration come next? Could it be that in addition to my other worries—the bomb, inflation, the possibility that the Reagan Administration would retaliate in some way for my suggestion that Mrs. Reagan trade one of her ballgowns for the Federal hot-lunch program—I had to worry about a sneak attack of cowboy onomatopoeia from within? As Minnick himself might say, "It don't seem right." As I thought that thought, I could hear the words of a C&W tune called "With All This Talk on Human Rights, Why Is It You're Still Torturing Me?":

Sure, it ain't right that them South American generals make some folks disappear.
But it's nothing compared to the flat-out suffering that's goin' on right here.
And the folks who disappear ain't nothin' but foreigners anyway,
Which is why you ought to listen when I say,
"With all this talk on human rights, why is it you're still torturing me?"

I had to face facts: That nitwit Duane Minnick might be a part of the swing to the right. Sure enough, a song came to me with the title "I'll Be Your Supply Side, Baby, If You'll Just Invest in Me." Supply side? Wait a minute! Minnick wouldn't know from supply side. Who's in there anyway—Duane Minnick or David A. Stockman? If Stockman's in there, I realized, he could be followed by Donald Regan ("He's Feeding You All That Bull, Honey, 'Cause He Wants to Get Bearish With You"). The dentist wouldn't be far behind. I began to soften my view of Duane Minnick. Sure, Duane has his faults, but as an example of the solid American yeoman class he strikes me as . . .

You bowled a strike when it came to me,
But now we're split, and I can see

Duane! Pure Duane! I listened with relief:

You used me as a spare, though it really wasn't fair
Then you told me as you left me at the door
That I ain't bowlin' in your bowlin' league no more.

The First Sixty-three Days

April 11, 1981

Some misgivings about the Reagan Administration that have been collecting in my mind since January 20, the Night of the Minks, were brought to the surface on the afternoon of the assassination attempt during the twitchy little misspeech on the order of Presidential succession presented to White House reporters by Alexander Haig—now known in Washington as Old Number Three. As it happens, one of the concerns was this: If General Haig is so smart, why did he finish 214th (out of 310) in his graduating class at West Point? Does that mean that there are 213 generals his age who are smarter than he is? If so, why didn't we win the war in Vietnam? Think about how many Vietnamese generals there must be who are smarter than he is. Of course, it's always difficult to make comparisons between disparate cultures, but according to my figures—arrived at through some complicated computations based on extrapolations of Pentagon body counts divided by cost-plus defense contracts—the man in charge of our foreign policy would have finished 845th in his graduating class if he had attended the Haiphong Technical Institute. The man who finished 844th, I am told, is now a street-sweeper in Namdinh.

I realize, of course, that there is no exact correlation

between class standing and intelligence; it is only as a matter of rough perspective that I find it helpful to keep in mind when dealing with doctors, that precisely 50 percent of them finished in the lower half of their class in medical school. Still, I have to admit to feeling a bit uneasy about having the State Department run by a man who was outperformed by two-thirds of his peers at West Point—an institution whose academic rigor was once summed up by its description as "the fifth best high school in Orange County, New York." My concern is hardly dissipated by knowing that the Secretary's number-two man, William Clark, has testified to a Senate committee that he thought Zimbabwe was a town in the San Fernando Valley, somewhere between Tarzana and Canoga Park.

Then there is the matter of what effect Mrs. Reagan's ballgowns will have on supply-side economics. David A. Stockman, television's favorite wonk-zealot, has assured us that when the income tax cuts go into effect taxpayers are not going to heat up the economy by using their extra cash to buy even more of the plastic doodads Mr. Reagan's principal supporters are trying to sell them. Instead, loyal Americans are going to invest in American industry so that, say, Detroit automobile manufacturers can buy some spanking new machine tools for turning out precisely the sort of car they believe to be appropriate for today—probably, judging from their past performance, something like a 1948 Hudson Hornet. It's perfectly obvious to me, though, that Mrs. Reagan is just going to take her tax-cut money and buy a lot of ballgowns. Mrs. Reagan has always struck me as someone who is strictly on the demand side. Her spate of ballgown buying, of course, will simply cause more inflation—meaning that the retired person living on a fixed income of a pension supplemented by Social Security can no longer count on getting a Dior original for $8,000, and will either have to dip into principal or eat cat food.

Little things keep nagging at me: Did the generals in charge of our military assistance program in El Salvador finish above or below Haig at West Point? If President Reagan intends to run the country like a corporation, could it be the Chrysler Corporation he has in mind? Is it really possible that I'm beginning to miss Billy Carter? Could that have been my voice I heard mumbling "Come back, Bert Lance—all is forgiven"?

I might as well admit that I find troubling implications in the personal financial problems facing John McAtee Jr., of Greenwich, Connecticut, who was chosen by President Reagan to head the Federal synfuels corporation at a salary of $150,000 a year, plus fringe benefits—a salary, he testified to Congress, that he would find it virtually impossible to live on. Giving us a clue as to how the Reagan Administration might define the phrase "truly needy," McAtee said that his acceptance of the synfuels job might mean that he would have to move out of Greenwich. What troubles me is the thought that everyone in Greenwich who is pulling down less than a hundred and fifty thousand a year might have to move out, particularly after the ball-gown inflation starts. I can picture them piling cashmeres and Betamaxes and tweed sports coats into their station wagons and heading west in caravan, like some preppy version of *The Grapes of Wrath*. What effect will it have on the fuel supply in the northeast corridor? How about traffic on the Merritt Parkway? Will the Greenies, like the Okies, all end up in California—so that a place like Burlingame or Pasadena might find itself glutted with more stockbrokers than it can safely absorb?

It may also be that I am still troubled by the pre-inaugural description of President Reagan's more belligerent foreign policy advisers as "a bunch of nuke-nuke jokes." Any fears I might have had along that line were intensified, of course, by the first public address given by President Reagan's national security adviser, Richard V. Allen Inc. Allen deplored the tendency of appeasers and nervous Nellies and that crowd to slip back into accepting the old "better Red than dead" line. Allen is, of course, entitled to make his own personal judgment on the *Red* v. *Dead* issue, but, given his proximity to the button-pusher, his statement made me feel like a passenger on a 747 who has just heard the pilot announce his intention to land on schedule at J.F.K. no matter what those sissies in air traffic control keep saying about fog and ice and wind-sheer. Given my own choice, I don't really mind being stacked up for a while.

Old Number Three

May 2, 1981

Washington, Aug. 16—It remains too early to say whether Secretary of State Alexander Haig's effectiveness will be permanently impaired by revelations that he summoned the State Department's forty-three ranking officials to State's executive dining room last Thursday at four in the morning to account for two missing portions of strawberries. For the time being, at least, the White House has sent strong signals of support by passing the word among Administration insiders that they are no longer to refer to Mr. Haig by the nicknames they have used ever since he showed some confusion about the order of Presidential succession while briefing reporters on last spring's assassination attempt—Old Number Three and Alexander the Grape.

For General Haig, of course, the revelations came at a particularly bad moment, on the heels of some difficulty he has had extricating himself from the impression that he was being disrespectful to American nuns killed in El Salvador when, in defending the junta's long-awaited report on the incident ("We conclude that gunfire was involved"), he again referred to them as "sisters run amok." General Haig has complained that the phrase was taken out of context—a complaint he has also made concerning the phrases "trigger-happy dames," "left-wing adventurers" and "Commie traitors." State Department aides, in attempting to defuse some of the controversy, have pointed out that Mr. Haig, a Roman Catholic, was brought up by nuns, though not terribly well.

Facts are just beginning to emerge about what took place Thursday morning after Mr. Haig discovered the strawberries missing at approximately 3:20 A.M. during what the State Department is now describing as "a routine inspection tour of the pantry." A few early rumors about the incident seem to have been disproved. General Haig was not in battle fatigues during the interrogation of his top aides, nor was he armed. The Assistant Secretary of State for Inter-American Affairs was not, in fact, forced to undergo a strip-search for hives; he was simply having trouble with the drawstring of his pajamas. All shortcake was accounted for. What was at first reported to have been foam at the corner of the Secretary's mouth was apparently Reddi Wip.

State Department sources have said unofficially that Mr. Haig had been out of sorts since late Wednesday afternoon, when what had been an extremely successful state visit to Washington by the royal family of Belgium was marred by a stern statement from the Belgian Embassy correcting any impression Mr. Haig might have given that he was in the line of succession to the Belgian throne. The State Department has said that the phrase that seemed particularly offensive to the Belgians—"I happen to be a Hapsburg on my mother's side, so la-dee-da"—was taken out of context.

The Belgian flap was not the only development at State

last week that Mr. Haig might have found upsetting. A strong protest was registered from Tokyo after American officials finally acknowledged that the ramming of a Japanese freighter by an American nuclear submarine last spring, previously called an accident, had indeed been part of Secretary Haig's strategy for persuading the Japanese to limit automobile exports voluntarily. Mr. Haig was personally embarrassed Tuesday when further inspection of the photograph he had confidentially represented as being "the secret Communist military headquarters" that justified the incursion of American troops into Guatemala showed it to be, as critics of the war had claimed from the start, an abandoned empanada stand. State Department officials are also telling reporters that Mr. Haig may have worked himself into a state of exhaustion, having recently shrugged aside the suggestion of anxious aides that he limit the time he spends posing for statues to four hours a day.

White House sources have also mentioned overwork in defending Mr. Haig, and have even made some attempt to justify the strawberry investigation itself—pointing out that Mr. Haig is "a take-charge guy" and that the Administration is publicly committed to eliminating government waste at all levels. Some Washington observers are theorizing that support from the White House is based less on enthusiasm for the general than on concern about who would replace him. The Deputy Secretary of State, William Clark, is said to have made enormous progress since his embarrassing confirmation hearing—after daily tutoring from State Department specialists, Mr. Clark can now name the capitals of all fifty states and find his way to the office three days out of five—but European confidence in Amer-

Truly Truly Needy

May 23, 1981

Still hot on the trail of precisely what the Reagan Administration means by "truly needy," we come to the case of Philip Caldwell, chairman of the board and chief executive officer of the Ford Motor Company. Yes, I know it was only a few weeks ago that I suggested that we had a promising lead in the testimony of John McAtee, Jr. of Greenwich, Connecticut, who said his salary of $150,000 a year as the new acting head of the U.S. Synthetic Fuels Corporation was so far below a living wage that he might be forced to move out of Greenwich. Yes, I know I brought up the possibility that everyone who makes less than $150,000 a year might be forced to move out of Greenwich—moving west in a station-wagon caravan that I thought of as a preppy *Grapes of Wrath.* Yes, I do still think of those poor Greenies on the road west. I figure that they've made it about as far as the suburbs of Chicago now. They set up their sad Greenie encampment outside Lake Forest, and try to make a supper out of a little cold breast of chicken and Chablis eaten on the tailgates of their station wagons. The men have tried to hire on as seasonal bank presidents, but they face great hostility: The people who already have jobs as bank presidents understandably feel threatened by the sudden appearance of a horde of

Greenies willing to work for $130,000 or $140,000 a year. When inquiries are made about housing—the mothers want desperately to get the pasty-faced little Greenie children out of the station wagons and into some place where they can get regular showers and a change of button-downs—the real estate agent says, "G'wan, we don't want your kind here."

Certainly the Greenies could be considered needy. Certainly John McAtee, Jr.—or, as he has long been known around the locker room at the Greenwich Country Club, Jack the Kvetch—could be considered needy. But for truly needy, it seems to me, we have to look to the executives of major American corporations. When the Reagan people talk about who has suffered under the Keynesian terror, the most appalling tales of atrocities feature as victims the executives of major corporations. It is the executive who has been seared by government red tape attached to his corporate body. It is the executive who has been brutalized by environmental zealots who would not even allow him to discharge his wastes. It is the executive whom government bureaucrats flail with confiscatory taxation until he no longer has the use of his own incentive. Listening to the Reagan people talk about the suffering of corporation executives, it is obvious why the President has said that the United States will no longer spend much time worrying about the status of human rights in countries we deal with: There is too much to do right here at home.

All of which brings us to Philip Caldwell, chief executive officer of the Ford Motor Company. For the year 1980, Caldwell received no incentive bonus at all—the main problem being, as I understand it, that in 1980 the company lost $1.5 billion. Well, you might say, Caldwell still got his base salary of $400,000—what the Reagan people must mean when they talk about maintaining a "safety net." Also, you might think it odd that I show any sympathy at all for Caldwell, since I was the one who recently proposed to American industry the Disincentive Negabonus concept—an idea that, I am sorry to say, got much less attention as a cure for low productivity than these fancy schemes like encouraging welders in Detroit to eat sushi on their lunch breaks. Under the Disincentive Negabonus plan, the salary of top executives would be tied not only to profit but to loss, so that for the year 1980 Philip Caldwell would owe Ford $274,358. Lee Iacocca would owe Chrysler Ford.

The point, though, is not my sympathy but the sympathy of the Reagan Administration people who get tears in their eyes when telling stories of executives who under previous administrations were forced to watch the public degradation of their smokestacks. I can see the Administration insiders gathered in the White House now, leafing through *Business Week's* Annual Survey of Executive Compensation.

"Did you hear about Phil Caldwell?" Donald Regan (1980 salary, according to *Business Week,* $846,000) says.

"Oh no! Not Phil!" David Stockman says. Stockman is from Michigan and he knows full well that some vigilante state safety agency, not subject to White House control, might have grabbed Philip Caldwell and made him submit to the mandatory insertion of airbags.

"He only made four hundred grand last year," Regan says. Everybody in the room knows what that means. They know that three executives of Union Pacific, just one company in an industry regularly announced as being too poor to carry passengers, made more than $2 million apiece in 1980. They know that the executive vice president of NL Industries, a company they have never even heard of (Could it be a Wall Street venture-capital group originally called No Loss Industries? A conglomerate built on a fast-food chain called the Nueva Latke?) made $3,225,000. They are aware that there are shortstops making more than $400,000.

"Will he have to . . ." Stockman stops, his voice cracking with emotion.

"No, no. He's still in Grosse Pointe," says Justin Dart (1980 salary, $1 million). "The cutoff point there is three and a quarter this year."

The room grows quiet. Stockman stares into space. He thinks of Phil Caldwell, trying to explain to his wife and children why he isn't up to earning the sort of paycheck that David Lewis over at General Dynamics ($3,012,000) or Donald Kelly at Esmark ($1,961,000) brings home. He thinks of the Greenies camped outside Lake Forest—the men gathered in little groups, discussing, in voices hollow with despair, whether things might be better in Shaker Heights or River Oaks or Scottsdale or Carmel. He thinks of poor old Jack the Kvetch in Washington, having to spend his lunch hour in Episcopalian thrift shops comparison-shopping Topsiders. Among those people, Stockman is thinking, there is one who is truly needy.

Trillin as Genius

June 13, 1981

When I first heard that the MacArthur Foundation was trying to find a couple of dozen citizens to support for five years, in the hope that one of them might produce a work of genius, I naturally started scheming for a way to climb aboard. I don't mean that it was the only iron I had in the fire. I had submitted an entry to the Reader's Digest Sweepstakes which made me eligible for a first prize of $100,000, with no obligation to subscribe. I had in my possession what purported to be transcripts of taps made on the telephone calls Prince Charles put in to Lady Diana while he was visiting Washington, and I figured I might be able to sell them to some West German sheet like *Der Stern* for a small fortune if the Boches didn't get suspicious about how often Prince Charles seemed to use the word "twit" in describing American officials ("You wouldn't believe this twit from California they have as Deputy Secretary of State, Di. He keeps referring to Mum as Queen Juliana"). Still, I thought the MacArthur Foundation was my best shot. I had read in *Chicago* magazine that the foundation was particularly eager to pour money on people "with intellects not readily defined"—which I interpreted as a cleaned-up version of precisely what my high school algebra teacher was always saying about me.

At first, I thought I would simply accompany my application for unconditional largess with letters of support from people who could testify to just how truly difficult to define my intellect has always been—something like "I find him absolutely unfathomable" or "I can't imagine what he thinks he's up to" or "cockamamie is the word that leaps to mind." I figured that the MacArthur people, who talked a lot about risking their money on the possibility of genius, would then see me as just the sort of indecipherable wacko they apparently considered most likely to make "discoveries or other significant contributions to society." Reading the *Chicago* piece more closely, though, I discovered that applications for the Prize Fellows Program were not being accepted. Names were being submitted by a secret committee of a hundred scouts who would never reveal their identity even to the Prize Fellows they put on Easy Street. The most innocent-looking citizen could be, in reality, an undercover genius-hunter—someone to whom I would have to give evidence of being the sort of breakthrough guy who, freed from the wretched bill collectors for five years, might just come up with a rhyme for Natchitoches or discover a cure for plastic.

"I'm reminded of a little experiment I've been carrying on in Nova Scotia on production levels in totally neglected apple trees," I said to a taxi-driver the next day on the way uptown, meanwhile sliding over to get a better angle for checking whether his beard looked real or pasted on.

"Eighth Avenue reminds you?" he said. He started

shaking his head back and forth. "Eighth Avenue reminds him of apple trees," he repeated.

Was he feeling me out? "The implications for the question of energy conservation alone are enormous," I said. "And the whole area of human sloth remains unexplored, I mean from a boffo breakthrough point of view."

"Is that the right-hand side of Forty-third and Eighth you want or the left?" he said.

Maybe he really was a taxi-driver, I decided the next day. I had shifted my suspicion to a plumber who arrived to fix a clogged drain.

"You're not the fellow they usually send, are you?" I asked, casually inspecting his clothing for signs that he might really be an assistant professor of comparative literature who, failing to get tenure at Northwestern, agreed to go undercover for MacArthur.

"He's out today," the plumber said.

"The poetry I've done—the indication of the sort of poetry I might be capable of doing—hasn't been widely read by the lay public," I said. "The epic poem I wrote during the Time-Life International Industrial Development Conference in 1957—'Ode to Combined Assets of Thirty Billion and Other Holdings'—was, in a manner of speaking, privately published. As to the sonnet I turned out during the same period in honor of my landlady, a certain Mrs. Krupevitch, a close textual analysis would indicate—"

"I think I forgot some tools," the alleged plumber said, edging toward the door.

"The area of social science is what I think of as my crossover field," I said. "It's in a sort of idea-generating dynamic combination with agronomy and the tango. My current project—uncompleted only for lack of funding, I might say—is an appearance/personality survey among white males age 30 to 47 on the correlation between designer jeans and wonks. So far—''

''Gotta get back to the shop,'' the plumber said. ''Forgot my whatchacallit.'' He flung open the door and vanished.

Was I disappointed when the list of Prize Fellows came out and my name wasn't on it? Who wouldn't have been? I had, after all, made certain sacrifices: The drain was still clogged. Also, I had just learned that the *Reader's Digest* had awarded its prizes in February without my knowledge. The Germans had indeed proved suspicious of the Prince Charles transcripts' authenticity. (''Aside from what appears to be an attempt to make the speaker sound English by an overuse of the word 'twit,' we find it impossible to believe that an American Deputy Secretary of State could have really revealed himself to be under the impression that the House of Orange is a California juice-bar franchise.'') Still, I did not join the chorus criticizing the MacArthur Foundation for having selected mainly established types who had for years been considered worthy of a flier by such long-shot players as the Ford Foundation and the tenure committee of Harvard. It might have looked like sour grapes. Also, I would hate to see MacArthur react by going too far in the direction of the noncredentialed: One of the Prize Fellows next year might be a cabdriver with creative ideas for an apple-tree project.

A Few Jewish Plots

July 4, 1981

I wasn't surprised to hear Callahan say that the Gouletas family had been invented by the Anti-Defamation League. Callahan, a loony elevator operator in a West Side apartment building I visit, figures that just about everything transpires according to a plan by the Jews. A few years ago, he tried to convince me that Sandy Koufax was an Irish kid hired by a cabal under the direction of Arthur J. Goldberg to pretend he was Jewish and thereby end talk of Jewish klutziness. ("Don't get me wrong: I admire them for it. That Goldberg's a smoothie.") Most of the tenants in Callahan's building are Jewish, but they put up with his crackpot theories because he's old and set in his ways and if he's upset he forwards their packages to Dayton, Ohio.

"You've outdone yourself, Callahan, you crazy old coot," I said. "If you're talking about the family of Governor Carey's new wife, they're Greek."

"Precisely," Callahan said, looking smug. "Very Greek. That's the point. For years, the A.D.L. has been looking for a way to correct the notion that Jewish businessmen are pushy nouveaux riches who made their money from shady real estate deals. Finally, they figured out how to lay it off on the Greeks. Watch. From now on, there'll be a steady stream of *arriviste* Greeks in the news—marrying governors, testifying before congressional committees about accusations that they've been forcing poor people out of buildings they want to convert to condominiums. Myself, I'm surprised the Greeks fell for it. The minute I heard of the Gouletas family I knew the Jews were behind it, but I figured they'd make them Puerto Rican."

"How does an elevator operator know words like *arriviste,* Callahan?"

"I read the magazines that the tenants get," he said. "During the day, there's nobody much here to take up and down. They're all out planning—using their clout downtown to have alternate-side-of-the-street parking regulations suspended on Simchas Torah, sending instructions to that Mrs. Bloomingdale they've got close to the Reagans to encourage Nancy Reagan to change her clothes eight times a day so American housewives will be inspired to buy more dresses from the garment industry. Close to the Reagans reminds me: What's the difference between a conservative and a neoconservative?"

"Could you just start the elevator, Callahan?"

"They believe exactly the same thing, but a neoconservative is Jewish and never learned to drive a car."

"Callahan, there are practically no Jews close to the Reagans. That crowd of Southern California used-car dealers that got him elected governor is strictly second-level country-club gentile. The crucifixion of Jesus Christ O.K., but Reagan can't be blamed on the Jews."

"That Reagan idea about the difference between authoritarian and totalitarian regimes came from an article in *Commentary,*" Callahan said, "8-G has been taking *Com-*

mentary for years. It runs stuff from that neoconservative crowd that used to be called The College of Irvings—Irving Kristol, Irving Podhoretz, Irving Bell—''

''The woman who wrote the article is named Kirkpatrick.''

''—Irving Kirkpatrick. They need one goy to turn the lights on Friday night. In the dark, neoconservatives begin imagining they're going to be attacked by black teenagers.''

''Why should Jews want to make a distinction between authoritarian and totalitarian regimes?'' I said, despite having just resolved not to allow Callahan to lure me into the conversation again. ''Even if there's a difference, both kinds push Jews around. Unless you're one of those people who think Jews are really doing well in Argentina.''

''Not as well as the neoconservatives are doing in Washington,'' Callahan said. ''I'm amazed that you can't see why the Jews started this. But of course you're the one who wouldn't believe that Colonel Qaddafi is really a paid agent Israel put in power in Libya to make everyone think that Arabs are maniacs—Operation Mishuganah. With big countries, the distinction between authoritarian and totalitarian is easy, right? A totalitarian country is an authoritarian country that doesn't have an electric-shock machine. But with some of these Third World countries it's hard to figure out, because a lot of them don't even have dependable electricity. And the ones getting American aid have to prove that they're only authoritarian because otherwise we won't send any more American advisers to teach them how to torture people. So they have to get the advice of people who know Washington and know how to split hairs.

And which people are taught hairsplitting from childhood in the interpretation of their religious writings?''

"The Jesuits?''

"The Jews, of course,'' Callahan said, following his usual policy of ignoring alternative theories. "Did you see Irving Kristol's article in *The Wall Street Journal* showing how easy it is for a trained hairsplitter to make a distinction between authoritarian and totalitarian? It's obvious that the whole crowd will be hiring out to get governments their authoritarian papers—the way people used to hire out to get actors off the blacklist. I'm surprised the *Journal* didn't make Kristol put 'Advertisement' above his article. I can see the notice on the bulletin board of the delegates' lounge at the United Nations: Irvings Associates, Authoritarian Certification.''

"I'm trapped in an elevator with a lunatic,'' I said.

"Jesus Christ!'' Callahan said, becoming so excited that he finally started the elevaor. "I just thought of a motto for Irvings Associates to use with some of those big torture countries: 'You pull out the hairs, we'll split them.' ''

"This is the floor I want, Callahan. Just open the door.''

"But I didn't get to tell you about the Israeli attack on the Iraqi nuclear reactor,'' Callahan said, making no move to open the door.

"Spare me that one, Callahan.''

He gave me his most knowing look. "The Jews were behind it,'' he said.

Literally

September 12, 1981

My problem with country living began innocently enough when our well ran dry and a neighbor said some pump priming would be necessary.

"I didn't come up here to discuss economics," I said. Actually, I don't discuss economics in the city either. As it happens, I don't understand economics. There's no use revealing that, though, to every Tom, Dick and Harry who interrupts his dinner to try to get your water running, so I said, "I come up here to get away from that sort of thing." My neighbor gave me a puzzled look.

"He's talking about the water pump," Alice told me. "It needs priming."

I thought that experience might have been just a fluke—until, on a fishing trip with the same neighbor, I proudly pulled in a fish with what I thought was a major display of deep-sea angling skill, only to hear a voice behind me say, "It's just a fluke."

"This is dangerous," I said to Alice, while helping her weed the vegetable garden the next day. I had thought our problem was limited to the pump-priming ichthyologist down the road, but that morning at the post office I had overheard a farmer say that since we seemed to be in for a few days of good weather he intended to make his hay while the sun was shining. "These people are robbing me of aphorisms,'' I said, taking advantage of the discussion to rest for a while on my hoe. ''How can I encourage the children to take advantage of opportunities by telling them to make hay while the sun shines if they think that means making hay while the sun shines?''

''Could you please keep weeding those peas while you talk,'' she said. ''You've got a long row to hoe.''

I began to look at Alice with new eyes. By that, of course, I don't mean that I actually went to a discount eye outlet, acquired two new eyes (20/20 this time), replaced my old eyes with the new ones and looked at Alice. Having to make that explanation is just the sort of thing I found troubling. What I mean is that I was worried about the possibility of Alice's falling into the habit of rural literalism herself. My concern was deepened a few days later by a conversation that took place while I was in one of our apple trees, looking for an apple that was not used as a *dacha* by the local worms. ''I just talked to the Murrays, and they say that the secret is picking up windfalls,'' Alice said.

''Windfalls?'' I said. ''Could it be that Jim Murray has taken over Exxon since last time I saw him? Or do the Murrays have a natural-gas operation in the back forty I didn't know about?''

''Not those kinds of windfalls,'' Alice said. ''The apples that fall from the tree because of the wind. They're a breeding place for worms.''

''There's nothing wrong with our apples,'' I said, reaching for a particularly plump one.

''Be careful,'' she said. ''You may be getting yourself too far out on a limb.''

"You may be getting yourself out on a limb yourself," I said to Alice at breakfast the next morning.

She looked around the room. "I'm sitting at the kitchen table," she said.

"I meant it symbolically," I said. "The way it was meant to be meant. This has got to stop. I won't have you coming in from the garden with small potatoes in your basket and saying that what you found was just small potatoes. 'Small potatoes' doesn't mean small potatoes."

"Small potatoes doesn't mean small potatoes?"

"I refuse to discuss it," I said. "The tide's in, so I'm going fishing, and I don't want to hear any encouraging talk about that fluke not being the only fish in the ocean."

"I was just going to ask why you have to leave before you finish your breakfast," she said.

"Because time and tide wait for no man," I said. "And I mean it."

Had she trapped me into saying that? Or was it possible that I was falling into the habit myself? Was I, as I waited for a bite, thinking that there were plenty of other fish in the sea? Then I had a bite—then another. I forgot about the problem until after I had returned to the dock and done my most skillful job of filleting.

"Look!" I said, holding up the carcass of one fish proudly, as Alice approached the dock. "It's nothing but skin and bones."

The shock of realizing what I had said caused me to stumble against my fish-cleaning table and knock the fillets off the dock. "Now we won't have anything for dinner," I said.

"Don't worry about it," Alice said. "I have other fish to fry."

"That's not right!" I shouted. "That's not what that means. It means you have something better to do."

"It can also mean that I have other fish to fry," she said. "And I do. I'll just get that other fish you caught out of the freezer. Even though it was just a fluke."

I tried to calm myself. I apologized to Alice for shouting and offered to help her pick vegetables from the garden for dinner.

"I'll try to watch my language," she said, as we stood among the peas.

"It's all right, really," I said.

"I was just going to say that tonight it seems rather slim pickings," she said. "Just about everything has gone to seed."

"Perfectly all right," I said, wandering over toward the garden shed, where some mud seemed to be caked in the eaves. I pushed at the mud with a rake, and a swarm of wasps burst out at me. I ran for the house, swatting at wasps with my hat. Inside, I suddenly had the feeling that some of them had managed to crawl up the legs of my jeans, and I tore the jeans off. Alice found me there in the kitchen, standing quietly in what the English call their smalls.

"That does it," I said. "We're going back to the city."

"Just because of a few stings?"

"Can't you see what happened?" I said. "They scared the pants off me."

Do I Know You?

October 10, 1981

As the leaves begin to fall, I still can't seem to erase from my mind the picture of Ronald Reagan at a reception for mayors in June greeting his own Secretary of Housing and Urban Development by saying "How are you, Mr. Mayor? How are things in your city?" I realize that most of my brethren in the Washington commentary corps have moved on to other matters by now, although the incident was mentioned by Andy Logan in *The New Yorker* not long ago and was used by *Newsweek* recently as an example of why people in Washington are beginning to wonder if the President might be what *Newsweek* calls "disengaged"—a use of the word that conjures up phrases like "she's really more than a disengaged blonde" or "it was nothing but disengaged luck."

For most of the summer, I was hoping that some witness would come forward to record for history the secretary's response. I still have no way of knowing whether he replied in a straightforward way ("I am not, in fact, a mayor, Mr. President, but Samuel R. Pierce Jr., the Secretary of Housing and Urban Development") or muttered something sarcastic ("Oh, things in my city are just fine, Mr. President. Most federal agencies are in the hands of looneys, of course, and the President doesn't recognize his own cabinet secretaries, but otherwise things are just dandy'') or simply panicked (''Jesus God! Let me out of here!'') or played along as if the whole thing were just one in a series of joke greetings that folks in the Reagan Administration use to amuse each other when they're not busy salvaging the economy by figuring out ways for rich people to depreciate their Jaguars (''Nice to see you, Count. How's the Countess? Did you ever get that little plumbing problem at the castle attended to?'')

I also have no way of checking the accuracy of a number of unverified explanations of the incident that surfaced during the summer—particularly concerning what Andy Logan's piece referred to as ''the dangerous implication that to the current President all blacks look alike.'' I can not, for instance, verify the story that the President in his Hollywood days got his shoes shined regularly by a locally renowned black man known to his customers as ''the mayor of Pico Boulevard.'' As it happens, I was told by another source that the Los Angeles man in question was not black, that he was the President's tailor rather than his shoeshine man, that he was not called mayor but named Myer, and that he was the man for whom the President mistook Murray Weidenbaum at a recent reception for leaders of the garment industry (''Fine, thank you, Mr. President, but I am not your tailor. I am the chairman of the Council of Economic Advisors, and am therefore not in a position to say whether a little taking in across the back would be advisable or not''). Maybe the President did greet Treasury Secretary Donald Regan recently by saying, ''another round of Pabst, Paddy, and some potato chips while you're at it,'' and maybe he didn't.

I have resisted the theory that the President has trouble telling black people apart because the only black person he knows is Sammy Davis, Jr. It is true that the Reagan people are always going on about how black people can pull themselves up by their own bootstraps without such Federal extravagances as a hot school lunch, but I'm not convinced that such talk was necessarily inspired by the fact that Sammy Davis, Jr., in his early days as a maniacally energetic performer with the Will Mastin Trio, was literally able to pull himself up by his own bootstraps—while continuing to tap-dance on his elbows and rendering "Lady of Spain" in the manner of James Cagney.

Just as I was beginning to stop worrying about the implications of this country having as Deputy Secretary of State a man who could not call off the name of the Prime Minister of South Africa, I had to grapple with the fact that we have a President who might not be able to call off the name of the Deputy Secretary of State. Then, suddenly, the economic summit meeting in Canada was on, and I could imagine President Reagan sweeping into the lobby of that old resort hotel they used, his entourage around him and his briefer at his left elbow. "That fellow over there," Reagan says to his briefer, indicating a man who is trying without success to hide behind a potted palm. "Isn't that the old duffer who's always dozing off during National Security Council meetings? The one who tried to get me to invest the Highway Trust money in that shrimp-boat tax shelter."

"William Casey, sir," the briefer whispers to the President. "Director of the Central Intelligence Agency."

Reagan stops in front of a uniformed man, hands him a five-dollar bill, and says, "Just have the luggage sent up to the room."

"I am the Chairman of the Joint Chiefs of Staff, Mr. President," the uniformed man says. "We are not allowed to accept gratuities."

The President smiles, and extends his hand to the Japanese gentleman approaching him. "Great to see you," he says. "Some beef teriyaki and fried rice this time. I don't like that raw fish."

"You're speaking to the Prime Minister of Japan," the briefer hisses into Reagan's ear.

"Well, why didn't you say so, Ed?"

"Mike, sir. I'm Mike."

The end of the summer was not made more relaxing by those stories about how carefully the President has to be briefed if he is to avoid striking those he meets as, well, disengaged. Now, I keep imagining Reagan preparing for a meeting of his own cabinet—patiently absorbing his briefing while remaining motionless so that Murray Weidenbaum can make measurements for taking in his jacket across the back a bit. "The wonky one's Stockman," the briefer is saying. "The one in the toga is Haig . . ." When the cabinet members show up, all of them are wearing the sort of name tags that are used at sales conventions: "Hi! My name is Malcolm Baldridge! I'm the Secretary of Commerce! Glad to meetcha!"

Longing for Bebe

August 8, 1981

My wife, Alice, was alarmed when she found me composing a note of apology to Hamilton Jordan.

"Is that the Hamilton Jordan you once said was the best proof yet of The Haldeman Rule that no nation has ever been successfully governed by advance men?" she asked.

"Yes, I'm beginning to think we were all a bit hard on him. I don't really mind a guy who throws a drink late in the evening now and then. It shows spirit."

Alice walked to the window and stared out at the garden. "You promised," she finally said. "You promised that this time would be different."

"I know," I said. "I tried."

"I kept telling myself I really hadn't heard you say 'Come back Bert Lance—all is forgiven' a few weeks ago," Alice said. "But you did say it, didn't you?"

I nodded. "I tried," I said. "God knows I tried."

Alice sighed. It was Alice who had persuaded me years ago to admit publicly that I had a problem—way back when Tricia and Julie Nixon made me wonder what I had found so dreadful about Lyndon Johnson's daughters. "It's a disease," Alice said then. "You have to face it: Sooner or later, every administration makes you nostalgic for the preceding one. Whatever you think of Haldeman and Ehrlichman, Jack Valenti is simply not going to come back to the White House, and you have to stop telling the children to ask for that in their bedtime prayers. Just a year ago, you pointed at a picture of Jack Valenti and said you had been too harsh on John Kennedy's hangers-on from Boston. You said he made you realize that the Irish usually make better sycophants than the Italians.''

''Marvin Watson seemed like a nice fellow,'' I said vaguely.

''Until the Johnson Administration left office, you always called him Marv the Snake,'' Alice reminded me.

''You're right. Of course you're right,'' I said. ''But this is going to be the last time. The Nixon Administration will cure me. There's no disease on earth that could make anyone yearn for John Mitchell.''

I really thought I was going to make it. ''Glad to see the back of him,'' I said, as we watched the coverage of Nixon's farewell walk to the helicopter. ''You too, Pat. No more Chicken Divan recipes from Tricia. Goodbye forever to Julie and that wonky Eisenhower kid.''

All through the Ford Administration, I seemed cured. I now realize that my symptoms were masked by the national relief over Nixon's departure. A few months after Jimmy Carter's inauguration, I looked up from the newspaper one evening and said, ''I sort of miss old Bryce Harlow.''

Alice treated the Bryce Harlow episode as the sort of isolated little spell that I could prevent from recurring by concentrating on the Gerald Ford Whip Inflation Now campaign whenever I felt one coming on. I tried. My will-power was simply no match for Billy Carter. Six months into the Carter Administration, during a lull in conversation at a large dinner party, I heard myself saying quite loudly, "One thing you have to say about Donald Nixon—in his own way, he had a lot of class."

"You need help," Alice said, as she drove us home. The Donald Nixon remark had broken the dam, and all I could do was slouch in the corner of the passenger's seat, talking about the Nixon Administration: "Sure Bebe Rebozo had his faults, but he did pull himself up by his bootstraps, after all. Member of the Hispanic minority, too. Which reminds me of the President's valet, Manuel. Good man, Manuel; loyalty's a trait seen too rarely these days. I liked the way Julie stood up for her dad at the end, by the way—right there in the *Ladies' Home Journal,* in front of the Jell-O mold and everything. You wouldn't find Julie appearing at shopping center openings, that's for sure. And say what you want about Tricia—you say plastic, O.K. plastic—but there was never any question of anything called Trishy Beer when Tricia was in the White House . . ."

As the Carters were about to leave Washington, I tried to signal Alice that I was confident of being able to withstand a new administration without looking back. In December, I returned from a trip to Savannah, where a little girl named Adelaide Scardino, age three, had done a splendid imitation of Jimmy Carter for me. "No wonder this country's in the shape it's in," I said to Alice. "Since 1976, it's been in the hands of a man who can be imitated perfectly by a three-year-old child." Alice said nothing.

A few weeks after Ronald Reagan's inauguration, I was becoming edgy. "Are you sure you don't need a picture?"

Alice asked. During the first weeks of the Nixon Administration, she had suggested that I keep in sight a large photograph of Lyndon Johnson displaying his abdominal scar.

I shook my head.

"I have a great one of Billy and his pals at the gas station in Plains," she said.

"I can make it on my own," I said. But I couldn't. The Reagan Administration had been in office only six months when Alice caught me writing the note to Hamilton Jordan.

"I was ready for all those used car dealers from California, but I really hadn't counted on Jesse Helms," I explained.

Alice stood silently at the window—motionless except for a slight shudder at the mention of Jesse Helms.

"Also, I thought Mrs. Reagan would stop smiling after the inauguration. I thought she was smiling because she was the only one who knew the secret of how simple-minded her husband is. Mrs. Reagan has been a trial."

"At least Rosalynn didn't walk around draped in mink all the time," Alice said.

"Rosalynn?" I asked tentatively.

"Rosalynn Carter," Alice said. "Pretty tough American woman in her own way."

I smiled. "Remember Mamie Eisenhower, Alice?" I said. "I really kind of miss old Mamie."